THE
SECRETS OF
PHOTOGRAPHING
WOMEN

BOOKS BY PETER GOWLAND

Gowland's Guide to Glamour Photography

Electronic Flash Simplified

THE SECRETS OF PHOTOGRAPHING WOMEN

PETER GOWLAND

A Herbert Michelman Book   Crown Publishers, Inc.   New York

Inquiries should be addressed to Crown Publishers, Inc.,

One Park Avenue, New York, New York 10016

Printed in the United States of America

Published simultaneously in Canada

by General Publishing Company Limited

Library of Congress Cataloging in Publication Data

Gowland, Peter.

The secrets of photographing women.

"A Herbert Michelman book."

Includes index.

1. Photography of women.   2. Glamour photography.

I. Title.

TR681.W6G68 1981   778.9'24   80-27504

ISBN: 0-517-541807

Book design by Camilla Filancia

10 9 8 7 6 5 4 3 2

CONTENTS

Eight pages of color photographs follow pages 116 and 148.

INTRODUCTION

Women carry the burden of needing to feel "pretty" in a world that caters to feminine beauty as woman's ultimate achievement. I am as guilty as the next fellow of seeking subjects with well-balanced features, flawless complexions and high self-esteem. These qualities make photography easy. I do believe, however, that much of my major satisfaction has come from photographing girls who require the benefits of lighting, posing and expression to accentuate their best features and subordinate the less attractive ones. Seeing added confidence in these models means more than the praise from a girl who is already aware of her beauty.

Amateurs and professionals alike rarely find a "perfect" model. One must always give thought to individual characteristics to determine how to get the best results. There is no one pat system to suit all. Of prime importance is the understanding of light and shadows. To me lighting is the basis from which to start, whether the source is artificial or natural, indoors or out.

In this book, I begin by divulging the secrets of basic lighting systems. For the first time I have diagramed the lighting used on every photograph. If the reader will read and reread, study and restudy the effects of the various methods, his eye will become readily aware of shadows and light *as the camera sees them.*

What emerges is a guide to placement of light rather than source of light. The source determines the intensity of the shadows. Whether you use artificial light or sunlight, its direction in relation to the subject will determine the pattern of the shadow.

The study of these shadow patterns is seen through photographs taken under studio conditions where light is easily controlled. The reader will observe the difference between a direct light and one that is bounced onto the subject and learn under what conditions a direct light is preferred over the bounce and vice versa.

Changing from indoor light to daylight, the photographer learns that the sun is like one giant floodlight and must be treated in the same manner. Its strong rays create the same harsh shadows as direct light in a studio. It must be tempered in the same manner when softer effects are desired. Several methods are explored: use of strobe, reflectors, sheets, black go-bo's.

Technique is one thing but execution is another. I've tried to emphasize the importance of planning before a picture session. It's like geometry—one does all the mental work *before* constructing the figure. I don't take pictures every day, sometimes only twice a week. Many of my friends think I'm not working when I don't have a camera in my hand, but the truth is that 75 percent of my photography is done before and after the pictures are taken. If one measures which takes the greater time, indoor or outdoor shooting—location photography probably would win. The problems encountered in scouting the desired settings, dependence on weather, finding models who are willing to take the time involved in travel and ideal locations for nude studies—all are time-consuming. On one calendar assignment we had a male and female model, two hunting dogs and their trainer, and two freshly killed pheasants. We had previously scouted the area, which was about an hour's drive from the studio. All things seemed to be going well, but by the time we had stopped at the pheasant farm and then driven another twenty minutes, the previously brilliant blue sky was becoming overcast, and before we could begin shooting, the bright sun was gone. The pictures were interesting, but not what the client wanted. Just one of the frustrations of working in outdoor settings.

Luckily much of outdoor glamour can be accomplished in intimate space rather than depending on wide-angle scenes. I've tried to point out how best to use tree-filled areas, warning of the pitfalls. Did you know that green absorbs a tremendous amount of light? What you see with your naked eye usually photographs a shade darker unless illuminated by brilliant sun. In a shaded area, ivy can reproduce as black!

Outdoor portraits give a unique quality unlike controlled studio setups. The reader will learn why I never use front sun for portraits and why overhead light is so unflattering. New techniques by master photographers such as Leon Kennamer apply perfectly to the glamour outdoor portrait and full-figure studies. His simple idea of blocking out the overhead light is explained and illustrated. Many of my outdoor portraits are synchro-sun, a system that can be confusing unless one makes tests with his particular strobe unit. I've tried to simplify the confusion over exposure when using this method.

In the chapters on studio portraits and studio glamour, the use of many lights and the use of two lights are illustrated by photographs of models in dramatic situations where each light is performing a different service to highlight a particular part of the body, and photographs geared to a more commercial market with only slight edge shadows for a postery effect. You'll learn where to place a light to emphasize a line or curve and where to place it to reduce a line or curve.

When I look back at my photography I find my best work is with a girl on the beach and with a nude in the studio. I like to be in control of my lighting when photographing the nude figure, because I am mainly interested in line and form as opposed to the sensuous, intimate personality. The latter are mainly for calendars and men's magazines, which require a completely different approach: more light on the subject, a personal friendly expression with eyes into the camera. Silhouettes and semi-silhouettes provide an endless variety, particularly with a dancer as the model. The reader is given the details of preparing special settings in the studio atmosphere, including the use of water to enhance the nude figure in a variety of ways.

For those who are interested in fashion I've explained the differences in clothing advertising for high fashion, catalogs, and local ads, and I have attempted to show the advantages and problems in working with garments, the fun of actually creating a situation and the chore of obtaining assignments in this really popular field. What kind of girl makes the best fashion model? You'll see that times have changed and today's girl is not the gaunt, aloof person of the past, but instead has a fresh, wholesome *young* look. And action has come to the fashion world. The technique of dramatic action as well as subtle action is discussed and illustrated. How does one make the model look as though she is 10 feet from the ground? How do you get a blurred effect? What is "peak" action? I've tried to explain in detail the manner in which these situations are achieved.

It's only natural that I've devoted most attention to the beach as a working ground. It is here that I've done most of my work and, indeed, where I first felt the urge to take photographs of women. The reader will find that an environment where there is a clear skyline and blue water provides an excellent setting for a variety of pictures in changing lighting conditions from the pink-orange of sunrise to the orange-orange of sunset. Here, the California Girl, my favorite model, is at her glorious best. You'll see lots of surf and sun and bodies in all kinds of poses from action to repose.

If you've come this far you're ready for some special effects . . . tricks, use of plastics, double exposures, darkroom magic. Anything goes. One never knows the exact result when straying from traditional methods, and that's what makes it fun. Many of the best photographs have been "accidents."

Read, enjoy and learn.

THE
SECRETS OF
PHOTOGRAPHING
WOMEN

Understanding and being able to "see" lights and shadows and how they affect the model is one of the most important requirements of glamour photography. Instructional material is often overly complicated, and many photographers labor for years without really understanding the basic principles. In the three chapters devoted to lighting techniques I hope to simplify the concept of light and suggest six fundamental positions, whether indoor or outdoor. Once these are understood all other concepts are merely variations of the same basic six.

1

DIRECT LIGHT INDOORS

1. Light is positioned directly from front, close to camera.
2. Light is positioned ¾ front, either right or left of camera.
3. Light is positioned at a 90-degree angle to camera, directly to side of subject.
4. Light is positioned ¾ back, directed toward the subject.
5. Light is positioned directly in back of subject, directed toward her.
6. Light is turned toward background.

The single light from the front produces a flat, shadowless effect and is excellent for portraits where the main purpose is to flatter the subject. This minimizes the size of the nose and tends to smooth the skin. While the front light position is excellent for the face, the flattening effect is not good for the body. One wants to see curves, contours, cleavage. The second position, ¾ front light, is one of my favorites to accomplish this end. How then to use the single light to the best advantage for both face and figure? Light the body from the ¾ angle and turn the subject's head toward the light. Some photographers prefer to light the face separately from the front by adding an additional light. To do this one has to use spotlights in order to control the lighting and isolate the area involved. John Engstead and George Hurell, two of Hollywood's top portrait photographers, are noted for this technique.

For dramatic nude studies, photographs of dancers, or any portrait when only half the body or face is illuminated, I use the sidelight (position 3) from a 90-degree angle to the camera. Depending on the effect desired,

1

the dark side can be completely shadowed or it can be slightly illuminated by the use of a fill-light from the camera position. This is probably the least flattering for general portraiture, but if your model has small even features, the result can be very impressive. Retouching is generally needed, for the extreme angle brings out blemishes and accentuates wrinkles. The technique is good for use with character studies.

The light placed at ¾ rear (position 4) is what I term the romantic light, because it gives a bright edge to the subject and leaves much to the imagination, as is desirable, for example, in a profile, a nude, a couple. Use with the nude figure is particularly appealing because the body is bathed in shadows. Even the lightest skin tones become darker.

Backlight (position 5) is generally a secondary light source, rarely used alone. Its main purpose is to separate a subject from a dark background. This type of lighting is frequently used in motion pictures to create an air of mystery—the subject is completely dark except for the edge light on the body.

Silhouette lighting (position 6) is probably the easiest to use. The background is lighted and the body is left in the dark. Its effect is particularly dramatic when portraying action.

The following diagrams and photographs illustrate these basic positions in varying combinations. Sometimes the backlight is used from above the model as a hair light.

The type of light used for all these positions can be quartz, flood, flashbulbs or electronic flash. The final effect on light density and shadows will be very much the same. In using color film remember that floodlight and quartz lights are compatible with tungsten film and electronic flash is compatible with daylight film. Flashbulbs are available for use with either tungsten or daylight film.

A single lamp is placed very close to the lens—either mounted on the camera or held near it, just above the lens. The subject is close to the background, thus keeping the shadows to a minimum. Many photographers use a ring light where the flash tube circles the lens. This method eliminates shadows on the wall. Model, Stephanie McLean.

BACKGROUND

DIRECT INDOOR DIAGRAM 1

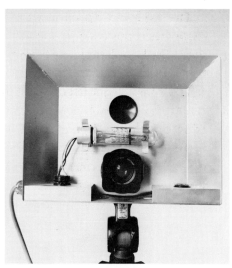

Homemade "ring" light using one Ascor tube 800-watt-second power. Hasselblad camera lens protrudes through hole. Top hole is so that the ring light may be used with the Gowlandflex twin-lens camera as well.

To obtain dramatic shadows on the background and give the subject modeling, the single light can be moved either camera right or left, somewhat higher than the lens. This gives a three-dimensional quality to the photograph. Model, Stephanie McLean.

BACKGROUND

DIRECT INDOOR DIAGRAM 2

To half-clothe the subject in shadow the single light is placed at a 90-degree angle right or left. If the subject is light in tone, a dark background is preferable. If the side light is prevented from hitting the background, then a light background is acceptable because subject and background will be separated.

BACKGROUND

DIRECT INDOOR DIAGRAM 3

A favorite method of using two direct lights is to place the front light ¾ to camera right (or left) and position the second light on the background on the opposite side of the subject. Such a placement eliminates shadows from hitting the background and the dark side of the subject does not blend into the background. Actress, Anja Brown.

BACKGROUND

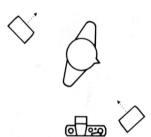

DIRECT INDOOR DIAGRAM 4

Two lights directed against a white background and placed so that they do not hit the subject give a dramatic effect. Water was poured on the terrazzo floor for reflection.

BACKGROUND

DIRECT INDOOR DIAGRAM 5

Classic figure studies demand shadows to accentuate body contours. By lighting the body from one side only and placing another light on the background the desired effect is obtained.

BACKGROUND

DIRECT INDOOR DIAGRAM 6

A single light on each side of the model with one slightly closer than the other allows for more detail but retains the shadows where most effective. Black background adds to the dramatic impact. Model, Suzanne Copeland.

BACKGROUND

DIRECT INDOOR DIAGRAM 7

Backlight entering from a 45-degree angle which barely spills onto model gives impressive shading to this figure study. A screen was used to block light from hitting camera lens. One light on background.

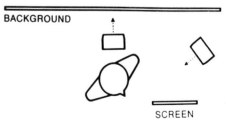

BACKGROUND

SCREEN

DIRECT INDOOR DIAGRAM 8

Another application of dramatic edge lighting. Two lights directed toward the model from behind and protected from hitting the camera lens by black screens lighten only the edge of the body and bring sparkle to the water as it splashes from the container.

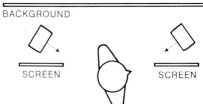

BACKGROUND

SCREEN   SCREEN

DIRECT INDOOR DIAGRAM 9

The light at camera right (or left if necessary) gives shadows to the subject and the light on the camera fills in the shadows. The intensity and distance of the fill light will determine the ratio of highlight and shadow. In this example the ¾ key and close-to-camera fill provide roundness to the subject.

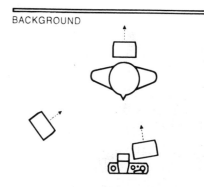

BACKGROUND

DIRECT INDOOR DIAGRAM 10

Not all subjects can stand this hard side light which accentuates the body curves more than does a flat front light. Two lights on the background separate model from background. Model, Diane Rose.

BACKGROUND

DIRECT INDOOR DIAGRAM 11

One key light and two lights on the background. The front light is placed to the left of camera, creating interesting shadows on the face and figure.

BACKGROUND

DIRECT INDOOR DIAGRAM 12

BACKGROUND

BOUNCE FROM CEILING

DIRECT INDOOR DIAGRAM 13

No front lights were used to achieve this soft effect. The two background lights overexposed the white background and the front light was turned toward the ceiling, giving just enough detail to the body to avoid a complete silhouette.

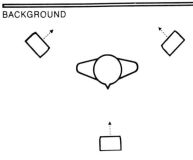

DIRECT INDOOR DIAGRAM 14

This picture uses the one-light source as illustrated in Direct Indoor Diagram 1, but here the models are moved away from the background and two strobes light that area. Models, Kathy Clark and Pamela La Grande.

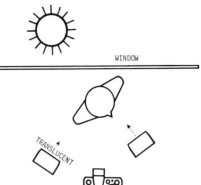

DIRECT INDOOR DIAGRAM 15

One main light, 1000 watt with diffuser over it, and a 600-watt light from right with barn doors to keep light off face. This 600-watt light also makes use of a dimmer (shown on floor) to keep intensity down. Daylight background from window.

The same principles that apply to direct light also apply to the use of bounce light, with the difference being softer shadows. Light that is bounced from a surface onto the subject is distributed in a wider pattern, and thus the shadows are less intense. There is very little difference between the use of a Reflectasol, a Soff Box or a Translucent for bounce purposes. In most of the diagrams I have referred to a Reflectasol—mainly for simplicity—but the result would be the same with a Soff Box or Translucent.

In bouncing light it is possible that color changes can take place with the use of various reflective surfaces. Daylight, which casts a bluish tone noticeable in shade conditions, can be changed to a warm tone by reflecting from a gold surface. Tungsten light, which is basically warm in tone, can be adjusted to daylight by using a blue

2

BOUNCE LIGHT INDOORS

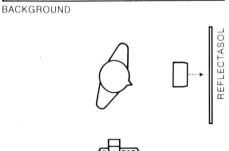

BACKGROUND

REFLECTASOL

BOUNCE INDOOR DIAGRAM 1

With a single wide light source at 90 degrees to one side, half the subject will be in shadow. Unlike direct light there will be a soft blending of highlight and shadow areas. This side light also illuminates the background. Model, Sonia Breeding.

reflective surface. An example of this would be photographing a model posed near a window, with the camera loaded with daylight color film but the subject lighted by the use of quartz light and some daylight. Unless the quartz light is bounced against a blue surface, the picture will be overly orange in tone. A blue glass filter over the quartz light would serve the same purpose.

The advantage of the Soff Box over the Reflectasol is that the light is contained within the box except for the side near the subject. With bounce from a Reflectasol or Translucent a great deal of light is emitted from the sides, which can shine into the lens unless shields are provided. The Soff Box eliminates the use of the shields and the problem of moving them continually.

Bounce light is like having a movable window. All the great master painters used it, particularly the Dutch painters.

The diagrams show the various uses and results of positioning these bounce sources.

Dramatic portrait lighting uses a translucent screen to camera right, through which the key light is fired. One direct light on the hair and one on the background. Not all subjects can stand this harsh lighting. Fiona Gordon's even features take it well.

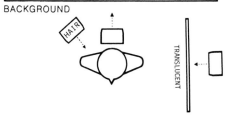

BOUNCE INDOOR DIAGRAM 2

A 36-inch Larson super-silver Reflectasol used as a bounce light. Strobe unit is a Larson Strobasol.

A quartz light is placed directly behind the model and directed toward the camera. It is positioned low enough that its beam does not strike the camera lens but does bounce off a super-silver Reflectasol which is positioned above the camera. Its soft light illuminates the model's face, thus the combination of hard and soft light. A Kordel star filter was used over the lens. The model twisted the diamond to bring out the most brilliant star. For this reason a quartz rather than a strobe was used.

BACKGROUND

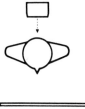

REFLECTASOL

BOUNCE INDOOR DIAGRAM 3

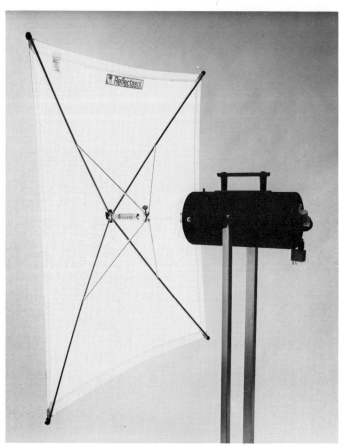

Translucent, made by Larson. This is a 36-inch diffusion screen used with Strobasol power.

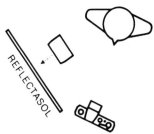

BOUNCE INDOOR DIAGRAM 4

Combining bounce light with window light. Here, Actress Joan Collins stands in front of a window through which sunlight is pouring. One light bounced from a Larson Reflectasol lightens the shadowed area. Exposure was balanced by using the correct shutter for the windowlight compatible with the f/stop for the bounce.

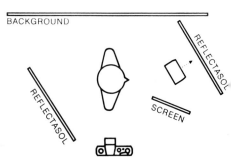

BOUNCE INDOOR DIAGRAM 5

Strong, soft light from behind combined with a weak front reflected light can give an interesting mood lighting. Screen is most important to block backlight from hitting lens. A diffusion filter emphasizes sparkle. Model, Diane Parkinson.

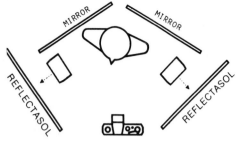

BOUNCE INDOOR DIAGRAM 6

Mylar mirrors standing in a V shape cause interesting reflections. An all-over flat lighting was made possible by using a bounce light on each side of the camera. They were placed as close to the lens as possible. Bits of colorful cloth were thrown over the lights to add a touch of color to the reflection. Actress-model, Melonie Haller.

The most flattering portrait technique results when no shadows are cast on the face. Shadows change the shape of the features. Here one light is to the left of camera directed onto a Reflectasol and another Reflectasol—right of camera—is close to the subject so that it picks up reflection from the first light and eliminates shadows. A second light is placed on the background. Model, Margo Johnson.

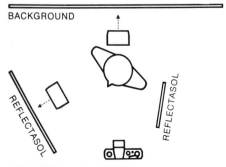

BOUNCE INDOOR DIAGRAM 7

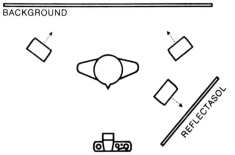

BOUNCE INDOOR DIAGRAM 8

One light coming from ¾ front gives dimension to this sporty illustration of Kathy McCullen. Two lights on background separate model and create a clear area for advertisers to add copy.

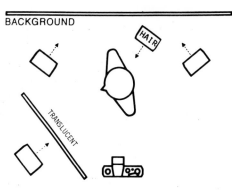

BOUNCE INDOOR DIAGRAM 9

Using the same technique as in Bounce Indoor Diagram 8 but adding a hair light and turning the model's face toward the key eliminates shadows in the facial area but accentuates the curves of the figure. Model, Fiona Gordon.

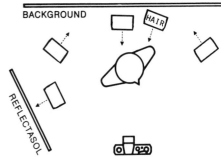

BOUNCE INDOOR DIAGRAM 10

For more glamorous lighting add a light behind model's head directed toward her. This gives a haloed effect to the hair. Kathy McCullen is the model. Works best with dark-toned background rather than white.

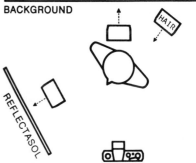

BOUNCE INDOOR DIAGRAM 11

Lighting setup for portraits or calendar close-ups such as Chris Hall with roses is the ¾ key Reflectasol, one direct hair light and one light behind the subject directed onto the background. Shield attached to hair light prevents it from hitting lens.

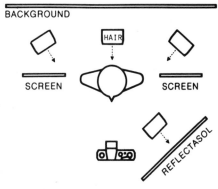

BOUNCE INDOOR DIAGRAM 12

Controlling skin tones on dark subjects is possible by using black background rather than white. In this case two backlights separate the model from the background while a hair light from above separates the hair from the background. The key light is from the front—a single Reflectasol. All lights were strobe. Actress-model, Roxanne Katon.

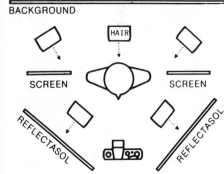

BOUNCE INDOOR DIAGRAM 13

Dark hair requires much light to bring out the contours and highlights. This technique works best with the use of a black or dark background as opposed to white. The use of two large reflectors from the front is the most flattering arrangement for portraits. The lights should be as close as possible to the camera. Actress-model, Karen Stride.

A 36-inch super-silver Reflectasol with a 1000-watt quartz light to camera right was all that was necessary to obtain this dramatic pose. Exposure was 1/500 at f/8 on Kodak recording film #2475 to bring out grain. The film is 1000 ASA. Model, Brooke Mills.

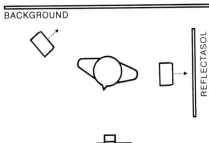

BOUNCE INDOOR DIAGRAM 14

DARK | TRANSLUCENT

BACKGROUND

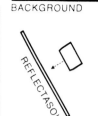

BOUNCE INDOOR DIAGRAM 15

Dividing the background between dark and light in order to obtain a light background on the shadowed side of the body and a dark background on the lighted side. The dark material is felt stretched over a frame. The light side is a sheet stretched over a frame. The background light is directed toward the model through the sheet.

BACKGROUND

REFLECTASOL

BOUNCE INDOOR DIAGRAM 16

Two backlights directed onto the model's hair are picked up and reflected back into her face by use of a Reflectasol placed above the camera and slanted toward the model. Model, Susan Hill.

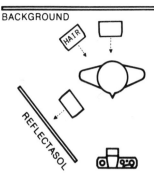

BOUNCE INDOOR DIAGRAM 17

Two hair lights, one from above and one from behind directed toward the model with a black background, separate the auburn hair from the background. Key light was low and to the left. Actress Beverly Jenden used this photo for commercial work.

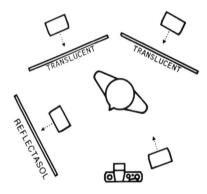

BOUNCE INDOOR DIAGRAM 18

An oily background look, requested by a client, is achieved by using black Mylar with one big reflector as a key light above model and to the left of camera. An additional direct strobe was used camera right aimed at her waist with a tube over the strobe to keep it contained on the waist area. Two Translucent reflectors were directed toward the black plastic to create reflections. Model, Lina Pousette.

Two Mylar mirrors 8 feet long and 52 inches wide forming a V with camera at one end of the trough and the model at the other. A single 42-inch Soff Box was positioned above the camera, lighting the trough and model. The mirrors bounce the light back and forth down the trough, making the effect soft. Single light on background.

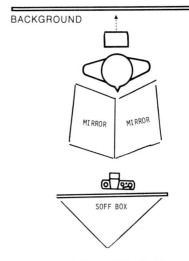

BOUNCE INDOOR DIAGRAM 19

A 42-inch Larson Soff Box with Ascor 800-watt-second power supply. The Ascor unit is twenty-three years old and is now used by five photographers in my rental studio. Speaks well for the product, eh?

Model is posed in front of a sheet of orange plastic. Behind the plastic is another black background. Between the two backgrounds a small direct strobe is positioned behind the model and directed toward her head. On each side of the camera large reflectors light the figure from each side and also cause large irregular white areas on the background. Model, Kathy Clark.

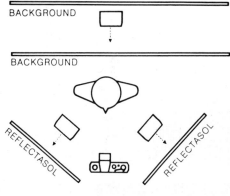

BACKGROUND

BACKGROUND

REFLECTASOL

REFLECTASOL

BOUNCE INDOOR DIAGRAM 20

In a bedroom setting with daylight coming in through ceiling-to-floor windows at right of camera, the 1000-watt quartz light was placed to left of camera, shooting down at model. Light was directed through a translucent screen made of of spun glass.

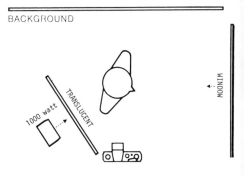

BOUNCE INDOOR DIAGRAM 21

Use of harsh-shadowed lighting for pose intended for the men's magazines is established by the use of a 1000-watt quartz light to right of camera and a 75-watt spot bulb in back of model's head, directed toward her.

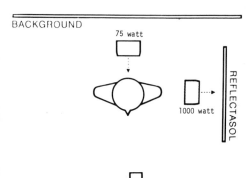

BOUNCE INDOOR DIAGRAM 22

Sliding glass doors were opened so that the camera could work outside, shooting into bedroom. A 1000-watt quartz light with blue filter (for use with daylight color film) was projected through a translucent screen. A second light on a short stand was placed behind the model's body to separate her hair from the background.

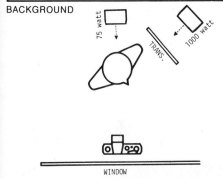

BACKGROUND

75 watt

TRANS.

1000 watt

WINDOW

BOUNCE INDOOR DIAGRAM 23

Use of two lights to produce definite, dark shadows on part of the body accentuates curves and camouflages the ultra-thin body of this model.

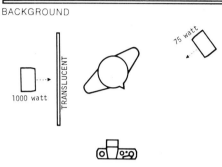

BOUNCE INDOOR DIAGRAM 24

The model was holding one light with her left hand so that it edge-lighted her hair, from back. The tip of the feather caught part of the light. A 1000-watt quartz light projected through a spun-glass screen lit the rest of her body.

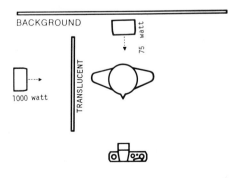

BOUNCE INDOOR DIAGRAM 25

Addition of a hair light placed on a short stand on the bed in back of the model and directed toward her hair separates her hair from the background. Daylight is entering through ceiling-to-floor windows.

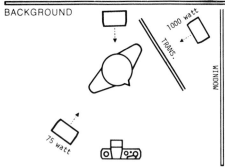

BOUNCE INDOOR DIAGRAM 26

The six basic lighting positions outlined in Chapter 1 also apply to daylight, with the sun as our light source rather than a flood, quartz or strobe. With daylight, however, we have two additional conditions: shade and overcast day. Under these circumstances our point source of light (the sun) has been diffused, much as with the bounce light, except that now the light is coming from the most unflattering position—directly above the subject. The small amount of light that illuminates the face is not enough to counteract the dark shaded areas, such as the eyes, nose and chin, for the main source is above. To bring light to these areas one can use either a reflector or strobe (or flashbulb) in much the same way as when filling in sunlight. Shade, being blue, is warmed by the use of a gold reflector.

3

DAYLIGHT

In general, avoid taking pictures when the sun is directly overhead. However, in this situation, pictures with the model lying flat with eyes closed, as in sunbathing or cooling in the surf, make the most of an otherwise unflattering light. Model, Kathy Morrison.

DAYLIGHT DIAGRAM 1

Variations of the sun as either the main source or a secondary source are shown in the diagrams. Sunlight can be used as a front source (when low in the sky) or ¾ source, backlight. In every instance except early-morning low sun and late-evening low sun, additional light sources will be needed.

For additional light one can use a strobe reflector. The reflector is inexpensive and easy to use but difficult for models to face without squinting. Strobe and flash eliminate this problem but necessitate calculations to balance it with the sunlight. As one moves closer to or farther away from the subject, f/stops and shutter speeds must be changed.

Early-morning or late-afternoon sun is easier for the subject to face. Shadows, while hard, are not unflattering as are those cast at high noon. Kathy McCullen is able to avoid squinting, but many girls cannot, even though the light is from a low angle.

DAYLIGHT DIAGRAM 2

DAYLIGHT DIAGRAM 3

The sun used as a backlight with no other source. A diffusion screen was placed over the lens to create a softening effect. This type of lighting is excellent for figure studies where shadows are desirable.

Action of dancing subject provides dramatic impact and emphasizes body form when captured in silhouette. Actress-dancer, Anna Neil.

DAYLIGHT DIAGRAM 4

With the sun, camera right, behind the model and a reflector at camera left, a soft look is produced in an otherwise bright and harsh lighting condition. Model, Karen Stride.

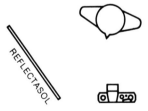

REFLECTASOL

DAYLIGHT DIAGRAM 5

For a postery, commercial picture a strobe is used to light the model from front with strong sunlight as backlight. Model, Stephanie McLean.

DAYLIGHT DIAGRAM 6

DAYLIGHT DIAGRAM 7

With the sun just passing the high-noon mark a strobe is used to lighten the shadows. Shutter speeds must increase as the foam becomes more brilliant; otherwise overexposure will result.

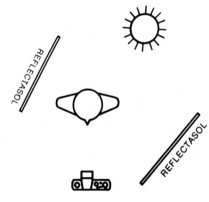

DAYLIGHT DIAGRAM 8

Using the strong sun on one side and a reflector on the other, two forms of backlighting are produced. The second reflector lightens the facial area. Model, Christine Burke.

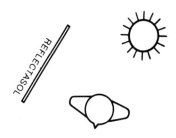

DAYLIGHT DIAGRAM 9

To create brilliant edge lighting the sun is slightly back and to one side of the model while a Reflectasol bounces the sunlight onto the other side. A Norman 200 strobe is the main front source. Model, Lynn Roth.

Sunlight pours through a translucent curtain creating a semi-silhouette. Exposure is based on a reading halfway between highlights of the background and the shadows of the model.

TRANSLUCENT BACKGROUND

DAYLIGHT DIAGRAM 10

Sun coming through a translucent curtain with a reflector used at camera right to lighten the shadows gives detail to the figure without destroying the shadows.

DAYLIGHT DIAGRAM 11

Two king-size sheets sewn together are held above model, Stephanie McLean, to soften the noon sun. Strobe from camera is the key light.

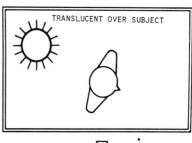

DAYLIGHT DIAGRAM 12

Only window light from camera right illuminates this lingerie pose of Sharon Carlson. Seamless roll of black paper was torn to make a hole which frames the figure.

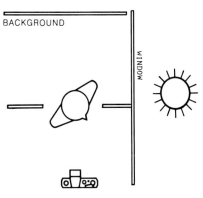

DAYLIGHT DIAGRAM 13

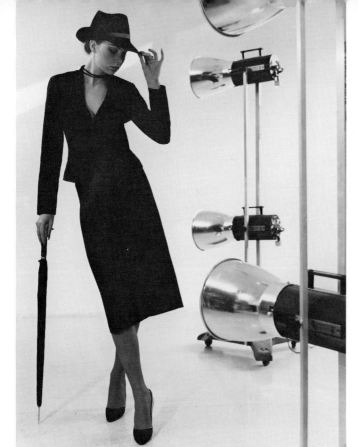

Window light from the right and a small quartz from front give this fashion pose the impression that natural light was the only source.

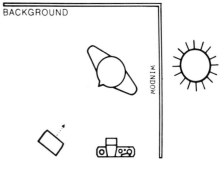

DAYLIGHT DIAGRAM 14

Window light from the right and a mirror used as a reflector from front makes flattering portrait of model Linka.

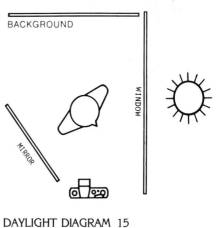

DAYLIGHT DIAGRAM 15

Blond model Kim Johnson is in the shade under the overhang of the ship's cabin. Exposure is based on the shadows which results in the background being completely overexposed with no detail. This is one method of eliminating distracting shapes in the background.

DAYLIGHT DIAGRAM 16

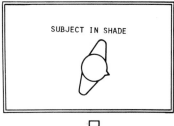

Same model and same location, but here an electronic flash is used to light the face and the background receives less exposure. Notice how the marina sights appear above her head. With less exposure, hair now appears brunette.

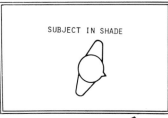

DAYLIGHT DIAGRAM 17

Placing a bare strobe behind the model's head when shooting outdoors produces this special effect, a technique used mainly with color when there is little sun. Hair separated from background with an edge light.

DAYLIGHT DIAGRAM 18

Taking pictures of a beautiful girl is easy. The actual operation of the camera, directing the model, deciding on composition and clicking the shutter are fun and exhilarating. Taking the pictures is the icing on the cake. Preparing for a photography session is another story.

As with any type of creative endeavor, the time and effort spent in planning will determine the outcome. Many photographers establish a preference for a particular technique and rarely veer from it. They may never leave the confines of their studio. Others work only outdoors. Then there are those who, like myself, work in both areas. Whether indoors or out, one has to plan in advance, to set the stage.

Outdoor settings have different requirements from those of the indoor studio, where lighting, props and backgrounds are controlled by the photographer. First, one has to find a secluded location, and that isn't always easy in this age of overpopulation and megalopolises. One has to drive for hours just to leave the city. But a beautiful woman photographed against a sylvan setting can be worth the effort when everything goes well.

I'm fortunate in living where trees, streams and waterfalls abound and yet are located only five minutes from the closest supermarket. I've made extensive use of all these backgrounds, but I still find myself imagining the excitement of working in more isolated, spacious, and exotic settings such as those in national parks and foreign countries. This involves finding a subject willing to cooperate for an affordable fee. New locations bring new ideas, as I found when I was in Australia and Hawaii.

Fashion photographers on assignment for clients with unlimited budgets travel to exotic islands, deserts and mountain resorts. I envy them, but only for their locations, not their jobs, because I prefer to feature the girl rather than the clothing! Better still, a slender nude or semi-nude.

There is a sense of urgency when photographing the nude in public places, for it is still against the law in most areas. One has to conform to a specific schedule, with time spent in prescouting to determine the best time of day for both privacy and lighting, and to avoid finding deterrents to a photography session at the last minute. Here is where the small-town photographer may have an advantage over the big-city fellow. If he is far from a

4

SETTING THE STAGE

An automobile serves as a natural prop for featuring the shapely legs of model Helen Harris. Daylight Diagram 6

major city it is possible to find isolated areas where privacy is possible. But not always—while in Australia we drove to what we thought was an unused stretch of beach only to find a peeping Tom lurking behind bushes on a cliff!

When photographing a nude model we take along an extra person whose sole duty is to act as lookout. This is a nuisance but necessary to avoid nervous tension and to avoid protests to the law. On occasion we have walked carrying our equipment, props and food for twenty minutes or more just to find a secluded stretch of beach or countryside.

We prefer to arrive on the scene just after sunrise. That means all equipment, props and food have been planned the day before and loaded into the car at the last minute. I've found only one or two girls who find these early-morning hours compatible, which has been a drawback in photographing in faraway places. The early arrival on scene is important, because the hours from sunrise to eleven and from three to sunset provide the most flattering lighting conditions.

With a pretty model such as Helen Harris it was no problem gaining the cooperation of aircraft owner to use his plane as a background. Daylight Diagram 6

Our locations are determined by our reason for taking the pictures. If we are working on assignment, our client has more or less selected the type of setting. If we are trying for the calendar markets, or want to fill our stock file, we have already selected a specific setting and subject. In the calendar markets there are subjects that the companies repeat each year: girl with flowers, girl with horse, girl with dog, nude. If we've selected the girl with horse, we plan to take several combinations, changing the model's clothes and the location, to increase the number of sales. One calendar sale is not enough to pay the expenses. In the case of girl and horse the animal must be rented from a person who will also control it during the photography. The model receives $75 to $100 per hour. If she does not have the proper costume, that is another expense. There might be a makeup artist required (although we generally use this service in the studio more than outdoors). If the final sales are made through an agent, there goes another 50 percent! So it is the additional sales that bring in the profit.

This type of subject is difficult in that one has to find not only a good-looking girl but a beautiful animal. All of this must be done in advance so that on the morning of

Jill Osborn is a gymnast, and that makes her ideal as a model since she is limber and can readily strike a pose in precarious places where many models would object. Daylight Diagram 6 (reverse sun)

the shooting there will be no delay. Time is limited when working with animals because their attention span is short. The background is most important to give the postery effect required. I look for an area where there is blue sky; a barn or fence also makes a good background. We begin with the horizontal format, using the Gowlandflex 4 x 5 or 5 x 7 camera. Calendar companies use 2¼ or larger—no 35mm. I will take only a few full-length pictures, because I find that the closer compositions sell more often. We change costume on the model, move the horse to a different location and take additional pictures. To finish off I will use my Hasselblad and/or my Pentax with black-and-white and color for some candid pictures of the girl with the horse and the girl alone. All of this may have taken only three hours; then we call it a day. The same procedure would follow had it been girl with flowers or girl with dog . . . always vary the pictures.

Many of the locations I've used for nude photography have been the homes of friends. I look for expanse of garden area where cluttered backgrounds can be avoided. I carry props whenever possible or look for interesting pieces of furniture in the home we are using. A chair, a stool, a swing—anything for the model to use as an aid in posing.

Improvising sets in our backyard or in our front driveway has given us the privacy needed in figure work. One simple setup that can easily be used by anyone is a lacy

I like simple backgrounds for a postery effect that features the girl. My clients sometimes complain of an oversimplification and prefer more clutter, much to my dismay. Daylight Diagram 6

The stream which flows in front of our property is a beautiful location. However, with the photographer facing north, the sun is always behind the camera. A king-size sheet is stretched above the model to soften the harsh shadows on the subject but allowing the background to remain bright. A flash is used on the camera to bring back the modeling to the body. For model's comfort and to avoid marking her legs, a piece of foam rubber covered with a green towel was placed under her knee. Daylight Diagram 12

curtain suspended on a pole with the sun coming through, giving highlights to the otherwise shaded body. I place one of my dark flats over the top and a carpet on the ground, and the look of a room is simulated.

When we photograph in the stream which is adjacent to our property we use two methods. If the day is overcast, the lighting is soft and requires no additional light except perhaps a reflector. But if it is a bright, sunny day, then the greens turn very dark and the shadows on our model are harsh. If we turn her back to the sun, we lose the waterfall effect, because it flows in the opposite direction. Under such conditions we place a king-size sheet over the entire area where she is located. This filters the sun onto her body but retains the bright sun for the background. By exposing for the shadow area, the dark-green background will be getting two additional stops. It isn't necessary to use flash with this type of lighting, but I usually use my Norman 200. The exposure is pretty much the same as it would be for bright-shade light. I don't stop down for the background exposure because the green needs as much light as possible. For example, if the background exposure reads f/16 and the subject reads f/8, I would stay as close to f/8 as possible in order to take advantage of the top light. To stop down to f/16 I would have to move the flash in closer, and that would make the shadows harsher because the flash would overpower the soft top light created by the sun coming through the sheet.

In winter months or when the weather is too chilly for working outdoors, I build sets in my studio. We are able to create a bedroom scene, a hot tub—whatever we want. Nothing seems to be too great a challenge. I'm fortunate in having a workshop connected to my home studio with machinery for working metal as well as wood. When I hire assistants I try to find young men who are able to work in the shop as well. My early experience around the motion-picture studios helped me to see how easily sets can be built. I'm constantly looking for props or pieces of furniture. I once found a rococo headboard in a trash bin. I transported it to my shop and sprayed it with white paint and have been able to use it on more than one occasion. I did the same with the front section of a catamaran that had washed up on the beach. We sanded and repainted it and use it as a prop. Creating an

A room setting (above and below) was created in our patio using a carpet and curtains. Sunlight pouring through curtains is bounced back by use of a gold Reflectasol, which is softer than silver and warms the shady side. Daylight Diagram 11

Semi-silhouette of Stephanie McLean is obtained by splitting the exposure between highlight and shadow. Daylight Diagram 10

Same situation but with use of flash to illuminate the body. Daylight Diagram 17

illusion is fun and has no limits. One does have to guard against putting too much emphasis on the scene and not enough on the model. This has happened to me when I've become carried away with a particular set. Basically one only needs to concentrate attention on a small area, for in glamour the close pictures, featuring the model, are best.

Working around foliage requires that the model stand out from the confusing background. Here Georgia Griffin wears a white doeskin outfit that goes well with the outdoor scene and she is further accentuated by the use of backlight. Daylight Diagram 6

Because our model's Latin heritage and long black hair give her an island look we used these elephant ear leaves, which matched the color of her bathing suit. These leaves were growing on the side of a busy road but by cropping her figure and dodging traffic we were able to make the exposure. Model, Yvonne Martinez. Daylight Diagram 17

The brilliant green of this overgrown Bermuda grass is a lovely contrast to the coffee-brown skin of Roxanne Katon. Roxanne's legs are slim, but we have used this technique to hide heavy thighs on other models. Daylight Diagram 6

A white framework was set up in our driveway and curtains draped over it to give a window effect. A white sheet over entire set softened the harsh sunlight. Daylight Diagram 16

This hot tub was built in my studio by
using 6-inch pieces of redwood and black
plastic to contain the water. My favorite
kind of figure lighting is when only the
background is lit. This gives a wraparound
quality of light to the body with a
minimum amount of detail and keeps the
figure from being a total silhouette.
Introduction of water gives that magic
quality that seems to go well with women.
Direct Indoor Diagram 5

This bedroom was created in our studio, because there we have complete control of our lighting and space to move around. The white-on-white effect was carried out to keep the feeling of femininity and yet not distract from the model. Bounce Indoor Diagram 9 (reverse key)

A high camera angle features a burned-out white background but was the only alternative to losing the model against bushes. It also gives a semi-silhouette to the body, which would otherwise be white and lacking in contrasts. Daylight Diagram 5

Close-up of model in pensive mood is
made possible by positioning her so that
the white hat is against the dark
background and her body is against the
brilliant sunlit field. Daylight Diagram 5

Privacy is important in photographing a
nude model in an outdoor setting.
Permission from a friend provided this
garden background. The interesting chair
gave the model a prop to lean on. Low
angle was to position her body against the
dark foliage with sun backlight. Daylight
Diagram 5

Semi-portrait of model Jennie Loomis, by poolside, is one of my favorite poses for portraiture. The reclining position enables her to use her arms naturally, and the tilt gives a casual look. Sun as a backlight lets the model open her eyes as the strobe illuminates her face. Daylight Diagram 6 (sun reversed)

This pool background could have been very distracting if the sun had been directed onto it. We waited until the background was in shade and positioned the model with the sun backlighting her hair to keep it separated from the dark background. Model, Karen Stride. Daylight Diagram 6

Preparing for a setting to illustrate a poem, two models were first dressed in white old-fashioned underwear with their hair styled accordingly. The day was warm and the pictures were candid, taken with the Pentax with no additional light. Overcast day gave soft natural feeling.

A man-made waterhole late in the day makes a lovely setting for this picture of Lyndie Shields in wet chemise. Pentax. Daylight Diagram 3

This is a contrived setup on assignment for a calendar situation. Red tub was rented from a prop company. Our dog was a last-minute thought. Susan Hill holds a piece of biscuit in her hand to keep dog's attention. Bounce Indoor Diagram 8 (reverse key)

Black on black using a jacket to conceal part of the body and two lights for added dramatic impact. Bounce Indoor Diagram 25

Photographing in a bedroom with daylight entering from glass doors, a quartz light is placed in front of the doors and a second light placed on the left side of the camera to illuminate the legs. Bounce Indoor Diagram 26

Men's magazines prefer the more intimate expressions and poses. Here the harsh lighting adds to the dramatic effect. Bounce Indoor Diagram 22

Professional portrait studios are leaning toward outdoor setups for a more natural look. New techniques developed in the studios are being brought outdoors in order to maintain control and produce flattering effects.

The first advantage of working outdoors is that it will give variety to the pictures. Studio portraits look the same even though the subject varies. Exterior locations provide a mixture of lighting and a selection of backgrounds difficult to create in a studio.

In portraiture I consider the choice of lens of primary importance. It is possible to make portraits with a normal lens (normal to your particular camera), but at a given distance it will not produce as large an image as will a longer lens. Moving in close with the normal lens leads to distortion; the nose balloons forward. I'm surprised at how many photographers do not recognize this distortion. They know that a picture doesn't look quite right, and when I've pointed out that the nose is enlarged they're surprised. The distortion can be very slight but enough to ruin an otherwise good picture.

A fair rule to follow to determine the focal length of a portrait lens is to double the focal length of the normal lens. For example, with a 35mm camera where the normal lens is 40–50mm, your portrait lens should be 80–100mm. I use an 85mm on my 35mm Pentax. With it I am able to get a frame-filling image of the subject without distortion. With a 2¼ x 2¼ camera, such as the Hasselblad, where the normal lens is 75–80mm, I consider the 150mm a perfect portrait lens (I sometimes use the 250mm on the Hasselblad). With a 2¼ x 2¾ camera (Mamiya RB 67), the perfect portrait lens is the 180mm.

How to figure the "normal" lens for a particular camera? Take the diagonal measurement of your film (in millimeters); that is the focal length of the normal lens.

Because these longer lenses require a longer exposure it is necessary to hold the camera extremely steady or, better still, to use a tripod. A tripod is the second most important piece of equipment for outdoor portraits after the lens. When you are working with longer lenses, camera movement is more of a problem. Also, you'll tend to work with lower light levels so the model does not have to cope with bright sunlight. At times I have used exposures of ½ second, 1/5 second or 1/15 second, and it's practically impossible to hold a telephoto lens steady with these shutter speeds.

5

OUTDOOR PORTRAITS

Stephanie McLean is posed against unlighted foliage background so that the sun, as backlight, brightens her hair. The Norman 200-B strobe was used on the shadow side to light her face. Turning a model away from the sun permits her to open her eyes in a natural expression. Daylight Diagram 6

Roxanne Katon, photographed with the same backlight technique. Daylight Diagram 6

Concrete wall is used as a clear background for Jean Manson. This time the sun is almost directly overhead. The use of flash fills the area of her face, left in shadow. It is best if the high sun does not hit her nose. Her head was tipped down to prevent this. Hasselblad with 150mm lens. Daylight Diagram 7

Under a tree the shade light would give a very soft effect. To add sparkle a Norman 200-B strobe was used. Models, Camillia Hudson and Tyrone Spears. Daylight Diagram 6

The result of soft light using Air Diffuser is shown in these two pictures of Joan Geletko. While she was photographed in the same shade lighting as Gowland and Cuadra (opposite), the strobe peps up the shade and puts sparkle into Joan's eyes. The bare strobe would do the same thing but the Air Diffuser makes the light a bit softer. Daylight Diagram 17

Leon Kennamer, a master of outdoor portraiture, has brought a new dimension to this field. Leon works in low light levels, preferring an overcast day or a late afternoon. His locations are woodsy glens. He always uses a tripod because of his long exposures, he sometimes uses the lens wide open. Leon brought attention to the unflattering effect of overhead light, whether it comes from an artificial source or a natural source. He blocks out this top light with black go-bo's (Larson Enterprises manufactures them) and uses reflectors to bring the light from whatever angle he thinks best. The result is absolute control. His subjects must remain still, since he uses long exposures, but the skin tones and surrounding colors are close to those of the old masters.

I very seldom photograph a model with the sun striking her face directly. Usually the sun acts as a backlight, which is very flattering to the hair. I use a Larson Reflectasol on the shadow side which gives a wide source of light. The most effective situation is working in partial sun or shade where the light level is low but the sun is available to fill in. The 36-inch Reflectasol folds up like an umbrella. I keep one in my car at all times because it is such an excellent piece of equipment for a variety of situations. Reflectasols are available in silver, super-silver, white, gold and blue. The one you use will depend on the brightness of the sun and the ability of the model

Peter Gowland with assistant Dean Cuadra in typical setup for making an outdoor portrait with Hasselblad. Cuadra is holding Norman 200-B strobe unit head which is diffused with an Air Diffuser made by New Ideas, Inc., 3728 W. Enfield, Skokie, IL 60076. This device can be carried in the pocket like a handkerchief and in seconds is blown up and attached to the electronic flash head, giving a soft diffused light.

to face the reflector. Most girls have a difficult time look-ing into the very bright super-silver Reflectasol but they can handle the silver or white with ease. The gold is very flattering to models posed in the shade because it warms the blue tones found in shaded areas.

In the bright sun I use a strobe and turn the subject's back to the sun so that she faces a darker area of the sky. Here her eyes have no problem with squinting because the flash is instantaneous, whereas looking into a bright reflector would make controlling her eyes difficult.

HOW TO FIGURE EXPOSURES WITH SUN AND STROBE/FLASH

The system for portraits with sun backlighting and strobe fill would be worked out the same as for the full-length shots. Strobe distances are established be-forehand by use of a chart made from tests with your particular strobe or flash unit at different distances. The background exposure is controlled by the shutter speed. The f/stop controls the strobe.

When the model's face is in the dark shade and you are depending on the strobe to light her, the shutter speed has little effect on the flash. This shutter speed is adjusted to control the intensity of the background, since the flash does not extend past the subject. The f/stop, on the other hand, regulates the amount of flash hitting the subject.

Synchro-sunlight (strobe combined with sunlight) is one of the most confusing areas for correct exposures because of the many elements involved. Every time the photographer moves closer to or farther away from his model (and the stobe with him), he must change both the f/stop and the shutter speed. One means of simplifying this is to keep the strobe at one distance by using a stand or an assistant. For example, set it at 8 feet for full-length poses. Then as the camera moves back and forth the exposure remains the same. For portraits you might decide on 4 feet. Keeping a string that is marked with different distances (or a tape measure) attached to the strobe, makes it easy to check from time to time to see that the strobe has not moved.

To balance the subject, Kim Johnson, with the harbor background an electronic flash was used. To wash out background an exposure for the shade with no flash would do the trick. The result is shown in Chapter 3. Daylight Diagram 17

Improvising a reflected surface by use of a gold racing jacket on model, Stephanie McLean. Daylight Diagram 5 (reverse reflector)

The result of using the gold jacket as a reflector. Hasselblad with 150mm lens. Daylight Diagram 5

On a heavily overcast day at the beach the soft side of the silver reflector was used to lighten the shadow area of the model's face. Because of the slow shutter speed the background became overexposed. Model, Debbie Shelton. Daylight Diagram 5

Long lens on Hasselblad is used to throw the distracting background out of focus. Backlighting with reflections on the tree leaves makes interesting sparkle pattern. Model, Susanne Gregard. Daylight Diagram 5

Use of a long lens again throws the background out of focus. Daylight Diagram 5

I'm a firm believer in working out charts and systems. There's nothing more dampening to the enthusiasm than to become confused and have to stop every few minutes to check on exposures.

In dealing with a full-length figure I prefer to use a hard light, because it brings out the modeling of the body lines. The harsh shadows on the face, which makes up only a small part of the overall picture, are not distracting as they would be in a close-up. I use the Norman strobe head at 8 feet.

Close-up of Karen Maybay by using Hasselblad with 150mm lens and 20mm extension tube. Daylight Diagram 5

For close-ups I prefer a wider source of light, using diffusion over the strobe or a larger reflector. One device I use is an Air Diffuser made by New Ideas. This is a balloon that fits over the strobe head, softening the effect. The Air Diffuser increases the size of your reflector from a very small head to about a foot. If you want an extremely soft light, the translucent Reflectasol in various sizes will produce an even wider source. One can put the strobe behind this diffuser.

Anytime you put diffusion in front of a flash it will cut down on exposure. I have worked out a chart for this diffused light just as I have for direct use. A self-sticking label attaches the chart to my power pack for easy reference.

BACKGROUNDS

Backgrounds for portraits must be complimentary to the subject, not too confusing and yet not so plain that they look like studio backgrounds. Never place your subject against a hedge or a bush. Foliage is probably the worst background, since greens tend to go darker in pictures. They absorb light. A means of dealing with bushy distractions is to use backlighting, allowing sufficient distance between the subject and the foliage so that the use of a telephoto lens will throw it out of focus.

Trees and bushes can act as frames if one finds a situation where there is a clear sunlit area in back of the subject such as a field, lake or grass.

Look for natural props that will not dominate the model: a log, a tree, a fence, a portion of a car. Props also aid in posing. We like to use the same techniques outdoors that we use in the studio. Getting away from the

Candid profile of model Debbie Quinn is caught during photo session. Natural light. Daylight Diagram 16

Suzanne Copeland photographed in two separate settings with sun backlight and reflector. Daylight Diagram 5

Use of sun as backlight with strobe fill creates snappy outdoor portraits. Model, Georgia Griffin. Daylight Diagram 6

conventional straight-up-and-down pictures, the model can assume a reclining pose, permitting her hair to fall free. If the situation permits, she can lie on her stomach, arms folded under her with her hands under her chin or at the side of her face, and other variations. These lying-down poses are relaxing as well. Trees with trunks that are not perpendicular often serve as seats.

It is possible in brightly lit locations such as marinas or beaches to find shaded areas where the sun illuminates the background only. Typical is the illustration of Kim Johnson (page 48) where we selected a portion of a boat that had a slight overhang, which protected her face from the sun. First we exposed for the shaded area of her face so the background received two or three times its normal exposure, blotting out any detail and giving a halation to the edges of her figure. Next we used a strobe to light her face and gave the background a proper exposure. Here her features were clear, the edges of the neck and shoulders were sharply defined, and details of the background were evident.

Both techniques have their merit. One has to decide according to his own preference. But this is an excellent means of controlling unwanted backgrounds.

Close to noon when the sun was almost overhead but slightly to the left of the model, Lou Mulford, a Norman 200-B electronic flash unit was used as the key light from camera left. Hasselblad with 150mm lens. Daylight Diagram 7 (reverse sun)

When I use the term *studio portraits,* I do not intend to imply that one needs a complete photographic studio, but rather that one is using indoor controlled lighting. A studio space equipped with lights, stands, go-bo's and so forth has the advantage of immediate availability, but it is possible to improvise a studio in a garage or in a living room. In my early days I did just that.

More important than facilities and equipment is the awareness of light and shadows. I can't stress this too much. One has to "see" shadows. Some experienced photographers still have trouble seeing what their lighting is doing to the subject and only when the pictures are printed are they able to discern the effect. The eye records more than the camera. For example, the photographer may be able to see eyes that are partially in shadow, but the camera may record only the shadow, showing no detail of the eyes. By squinting one is better able to determine approximately what the camera sees.

An excellent program for learning to "see" shadows and light is to practice with the use of one floodlight. Position it directly on camera (slightly above rather than below) and move the light slowly to one side of the model

6

STUDIO PORTRAITS

My favorite portrait lighting . . . very flattering. Two homemade 16 x 48-inch light boxes, one on each side of the Hasselblad. The 800-watt-second Ascor power tubes face back and bounce forward. Bulbs shown are for pilots. Can be used as the main light instead of strobe if you wish.

and then the other. Shadows made with this hard source are readily noticeable because they are harsh and definite. I find the most flattering position is generally from the camera angle. This is a commercial, flat type of lighting which casts the least amount of shadow on the facial plane. Beautiful pictures can be made with just one light. The reason for additional sources is not to change the basic effect of the single light, but to embellish it; to eliminate the shadow cast on the background, to lighten the hair. The photographer notes where the shadow falls on the background and then directs the light onto it from the opposite side of the single light. A third light, used on a boom above the model's head and directed onto her hair, will add brilliant highlights and separate the hair from the background. The hair light should be brought in from one side or the other rather than directly above her head. Be careful that it does not strike any part of her face. Sometimes it is necessary to form a piece of cardboard or heavy paper around a part of the light to keep it from hitting the camera lens and to restrict it to the hair area.

Two-box technique. Note low light to wash out shadows. Also note two catch lights in eyes. One bare Ascor flash tube was placed behind the model's head and one 200-watt-second slave hair light overhead.

The placement of the original "key" light can change the shape of the face. Professional models generally do not require modified lighting. They should be photogenic from any angle. However, for dramatic effect the face can be placed in half shadow by placing the "key" light completely to one side of the subject. Here the use of a fourth light is optional depending on whether or not any detail is desired on the shadowed side. Used in this manner, the fourth light is a "fill." One would not want the same density of light hitting the shadow area as is hitting the lighted side. The ratio should be about 2 to 1. Controlling the intensity of the light can be done in several ways. It can be moved farther away, or one can place a translucent screen in front of it. Larson Enterprises makes the Translucent Reflectasols for this purpose.

The main point that I am trying to make is that lighting of the face with a single source should create the basic effect that is desired. Any additional lights should not cast conflicting shadows but only lighten those already there, add highlights to the hair and eliminate shadows from the background. An endless combination of possibilities exists.

What about flash or strobe lights? How can one tell what the light will be doing? You can't unless you use a

Same technique using only one box. Note single catch light in eyes.

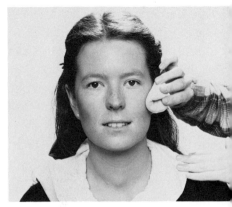

Chris Merriman without benefit of makeup or hair styling. Bounce Indoor Diagram 9

Liquid foundation is first applied and then powdered. Bounce Indoor Diagram 9

Eyelids are shaded at corners and mascara applied to lashes. Bounce Indoor Diagram 9

Rouge has been applied to cheeks; lipstick of a neutral color is shaped to lips and then blotted before covering with clear gloss. Freckles have been individually touched with a small brush and "Erase." Bounce Indoor Diagram 9

With hair curled and styled, and a black background to accentuate the lighted hair, Chris is now a different girl. Bounce Indoor Diagram 12

"pilot" light from the same position as the strobe. Many strobe units have built-in pilot lights, but frequently they are not strong enough to determine the effect. (See "Studio Glamour," Chapter 7.) I have attached a 650-watt light on a dimmer to the stem that holds my strobe. The strobe is pointed at my 72-inch Hex Reflectasol, but the 650-watt is pointed at the model. I use the dimmer system because if the model's eyes are sensitive, the brightness may cause squinting. I use the strongest power only to focus and then dim it for comfort.

The placement of a single light, whether it be bounce or direct, will produce the same shadow pattern on your model. The only difference will be that the bounce light produces a softer set of shadows.

One of my favorite glamour portraits is with the use of four lights directed toward the model from behind her. The background is black. One broad source from slightly right or left of camera lights the face. The lens is protected from the four backlights by use of black flats on stands. On brunettes this is particularly effective because it gives a haloed edge separating the hair from the

Model-actress Linka has a quiet, petulant quality that lends itself well to this soft window light. Hasselblad. Daylight Diagram 15

Subject is standing next to a floor-to-ceiling opaque glass window. A mirror on wheels is reflecting light onto the shaded side of face. Daylight Diagram 14

background. With blondes the lights need not be so intense.

The placement of the main front light will depend on the subject. Study the features closely. Not all girls can take extreme side lighting. Any irregularities in the shape of the nose will be accentuated. You'll find that long, thin faces look better from a front view rather than a ¾ view, because they usually lack prominent cheekbones. Turning the thin face to the ¾ position produces a shape lacking in curves and can make the nose look large. Perhaps that is why most of the successful models have prominent cheekbones. Makeup artists have always used shadowing on the side of the face just under the cheekbone to accentuate or to produce a curved look where one is lacking. It seems to work successfully when done with skill, but too often my models apply this shading looking only from the front view. When their faces are turned to the side, unflattering dark blotches appear. I don't like the overuse of makeup on any part of the face, and even when a professional makeup artist is on hand I find that I often have to ask him to modify a particular area. It is very important for the aspiring model to learn how to apply her own makeup. It is interesting to see the progress made by girls who have never worn makeup and then take a course in how to apply it. First they are apt to exaggerate and experiment with every new product that comes along. Finally they reach a point of moderation where one is not aware of the cosmetics, and that is the way I prefer my models to look. There are times when a particular product requires the garish look of the femme fatale, and then playing with various colors, shadings and glosses can be fun.

The combination of makeup and retouching brings back memories of the Hollywood portrait photographers. Even the youngest, most unblemished faces were smoothed out by the retoucher's pencil, giving an artificial angelic quality. Today's retouchers have modified their techniques so that at times one cannot readily detect that the picture has been worked on. A little retouching helps almost any portrait.

One problem in using the 35mm camera for portrait work is that the negative is too small for retouching. In this case one can use diffusion screens. There are professional glass diffusers that fit over the lens, and there are improvised means of creating a soft look to the negative. A fine piece of netting with a hole burned in the center is what I've used for years. One can experiment with different methods or fabrics. One photographer tells me he has great luck with a piece of nylon hose stretched over a frame. Sometimes the use of net has an advantage in that it does not produce a double image around the person as the glass filters do.

The option to retouch both color and black-and-white

With the model illuminated only by the amount of light that reflects off the background, the poses for portraits require a profile or ¾ angle of the body. Hasselblad with 150mm. Direct Indoor Diagram 5

Actress Brooke Mills's lovely profile and sensuous mood are captured by the use of one 600-watt quartz light bounced off a silver Reflectasol. Head hides light from camera. Bounce Indoor Diagram 3

Using the '40s technique of placing the model in a reclining position with camera shooting down creates a glamorous mood and accentuates beautiful hair. Model-actress, Lee Ann Duffield. Bounce Indoor Diagram 1

negatives is one of the reasons I use the Gowlandflex camera. It takes the larger (4 x 5) negative. I've also had portraits from the Hasselblad negative (2¼ x 2¼) re-touched, but in most cases I've used the telephoto lens to provide a big image that fills the frame. An advantage of the larger negatives is that they can be retouched with a lead pencil without the application of retouching fluid. The larger negatives are manufactured with a semi-rough surface which is called "tooth" so that the lead pencil sticks easily. The smaller roll film, however, is slick so that it will not scratch easily and thus the lead does not stick unless a fluid is used first.

The cost of retouching a black-and-white negative is unbelievably cheap, and retouching color negatives can be done at a fairly reasonable cost. Retouching color transparencies is a much more expensive procedure. The work on a transparency requires the use of dyes while the work on both black-and-white and color nega-tives is done with pencils.

Lighting, makeup, retouching—all of these are im-portant, but without the benefit of a good expression on the model they're useless. So knowing how to make the subject relax and feel natural in front of the camera is just as necessary as knowing the technical aspects of work-ing camera and lights.

The personality of the photographer has a lot to do

with bringing a casual feeling to the subject. If he or she is not completely at home with the equipment, and not sure of what steps to take in correcting lighting or pose, then the subject feels this and can become tense. I've found that if humor is applied, tensions relax. I've known glamour photographers who become temperamental over trivial matters. I suppose they're recalling something they read or heard about artists being emotional. I prefer to keep things light. With some of my toughest 8 x 10 assignments, where technical problems can be irritating, I try to keep a patter of conversation going so that I and my assistant are the only ones aware of any problem. My wife, Alice, offers cheese, crackers, soft drinks, wine . . . and that helps any tension.

Astrology has been one of my hobbies, and I use it to a great extent when meeting new subjects. Talking about politics or religion can stir violent emotions, but astrology is fun. I find that I can get a laugh out of the most nervous model just by telling her something about herself. I ask about her boyfriend. "What sign is he?" Invariably I'll tell her that's a terrible sign for her, and that gets an immediate response. She's already forgetting her tensions.

Expressive eyes are important to the world of modeling. Here, Camille Sutton's warm engaging look is the focus of a striking portrait. Hasselblad. Bounce Indoor Diagram 12

Small white Christmas lights were poked through a black paper background and with the use of long lens created irregular bright circles. A combination of window light (camera right) and a quartz bounced against a Reflectasol (camera left). Dimmer was used on quartz to bring the light to the low level of the soft daylight. Bounce Indoor Diagram 21

I never flatter a girl unless I mean it. When I've looked into the camera for a while and I begin to notice one feature over another, I comment on that feature. Anyone in front of a camera is self-conscious and concerned about how she looks, even pretty models. I should say *particularly* pretty models. They need constant reassurance.

Another method of achieving relaxed and natural expressions is through posing. I rarely use conventional methods such as sitting in a chair or on a bench. When I use those props I have my subjects lean or lie on them.

With the model on her stomach, her body profile to the camera, she can prop herself up with her arms, turn her head toward the camera, lean her head to the side so that

Kathy McCullen, a successful model, need only show half her face to charm the camera. Her healthy vibrancy comes through with only one eye showing. Bounce Indoor Diagram 9

Dark skin tones are more accurately controlled when black backgrounds with much backlight are used. Here, lovely Roxanne Katon expresses both moody and happy feelings. Bounce Indoor Diagram 12

Jennifer Loomis is able either to look unsophisticated with hair loose and big smile . . .

. . . or, with hair back and change of expression, to appear stylish and mature. Bounce Indoor Diagram 9 (key reversed)

her hair falls free, lower her arms, cross them in front of her and place her chin lightly on them, use her hands next to her cheeks or under the chin. The poses are endless and all most flattering. Something about this position is good for neck- and chinlines. If you are using a 35mm camera it is better to position the subject on a high table, otherwise you'll find yourself on your stomach as well. Using the Gowlandflex, with which I can view the image from above, does not present this problem. While on the floor the model can also turn onto her back with her hair flaring out around her and the photographer can shoot down at an angle.

My new studio Swing Light is excellent for this type of work, since the large hex can be positioned easily above the subject without wires and stand legs getting in the way.

Another pose that I use for portraits is bending over a stool from a standing position, arms down, hands on the stool. This also is excellent for neck- and chinlines and lets the hair hang free in a flattering manner. I've rarely found this pose to be unattractive.

In my studio is a mirror on a stand that can be tipped up or down. The models find this to be a great help in

Actress Brooke Mills's even features and raven hair emphasize her glamorous quality, here embellished by the use of many backlights. The retoucher, Loretta Jackson of Santa Monica, skillfully avoided exaggerated retouching on this 2¼ x 2¼ negative. Bounce Indoor Diagram 12

posing themselves or in following any of my instructions. The mirror is 30 x 40 inches and is on wheels so that it can be moved about easily. If Alice is arranging the model's hair she can look into the mirror and see what the camera will see. I've also photographed from over the top of the mirror so my subject sees herself as the camera sees her. Occasionally a girl will ask to have the mirror removed because it makes her nervous, and then sometimes girls shift their eyes at the last minute to catch a glimpse of themselves. But on the whole it is a great idea and I've been using it for thirty years!

Allison Davies, a talented actress, was kind enough to permit publication of this photograph taken without benefit of makeup or hair styling or thought of pose or expression—a quick, candid picture. Bounce Indoor Diagram 11

A change of face angle, with makeup applied and hair curled and brushed, and a more accurate picture of Allison is possible. Still the slightly rough skin areas are noticeable. Bounce Indoor Diagram 11

*With the help of retouching, possible on
2¼ and larger negatives but not on 35mm,
Allison is given the glamorous appearance
that she radiates in person. Hasselblad.
Bounce Indoor Diagram 11*

The principles of working indoors are much the same as those of working outdoors. A hard key light from a single spot or quartz or small photoflood in a studio is similar to working with sunlight; it comes from a single point source. Soft lighting such as bounce light or translucent is much like shade or working on an overcast day when the light comes from a wide source.

Hard lighting is used for specific purposes in bringing out character or texture by accentuating the shadow areas. We see this type used with portraits of Indian chiefs or fabrics such as burlap. The opposite is true with soft light. Here you want to minimize texture or wrinkles either on the face or clothing. The softer the light the better.

In a studio the photographer has a choice of using a spotlight as the hard source or a reflector for the soft effect.

Available today are the umbrella-type reflectors. The most popular is the 36-inch Larson Reflectasol. It comes in surfaces ranging from white to soft silver to super-silver. Also available are gold or blue for special occasions. For a small studio and close-up work the 36-inch Reflectasol or the 36-inch Translucent is adequate.

In my studio I have found that the 72-inch Larson Hex Reflectasol has an advantage over the smaller one in that it gives a much wider, softer light source and can be used for full-lengths as well as for close-ups.

Over the years I have designed several ways of suspending this light. First I had it on a stand which moved around the studio, and later I hung one Hex on each side of the studio so that I could change the key light from one side to the other. I have now gone back to the use of a single 72-inch Hex umbrella (super-silver), which is on a boom that swivels over the model's head in an 18-foot circle. It can be raised and lowered by the use of counterbalanced steel cables.

Anyone with a 10-foot ceiling should look into this, because the absence of wiring on the floor and the ease with which the light can be moved makes it possible to change quickly from one type of lighting to another.

One of the disadvantages of bounce lighting is that one cannot usually see the effect of the lighting on the subject because the intensity of the pilot light bounced against the reflector and onto the model is too weak. To solve this problem we have mounted a 650-watt quartz movie light in front of the strobe's reflector directed

7

STUDIO GLAMOUR

With available light only, this model was caught spontaneously while making adjustment to her costume. Light from window at one side creates pleasing contours to the body and gives a silvery look to the blond hair. Kodak 2475 recording film (1000 ASA) gives grainy effect. Daylight Diagram 13

toward the subject. This light is wired on a dimmer in the strobe so that its intensity can be raised and lowered according to the ability of the model to cope with the light. Some girls can stand a brighter light than others.

Many photographers prefer the translucent system where the strobe light is softened and broadened by the use of translucent material. The degree of softness will depend on the size of the translucent. One such system is a light called the Soff Box, developed by George Larson. It is a square light that comes in 17-inch, 25-inch and 42-inch sizes. The advantage of this system is that the strobe is contained within the box and directed at the model through the translucent material. With the reflector system the photographer must always guard against the strobe hitting his lens, since it is directed away from the model at the reflector. If the light is next to the camera

Postery effect where model stands out against plain background area using 800-watt Norman strobe with 72-inch Larson Hex and four Strobasols on background. Pose emphasizes shapely legs of model Anja Brown. Bounce Indoor Diagram 9 (reverse key)

Popular technique for fashion work is the use of a single hard light source creating either a slight shadow or a deep shadow depending on placement of the light. Helen Harris wet her hair for this bathing-suit illustration. Direct Indoor Diagram 1

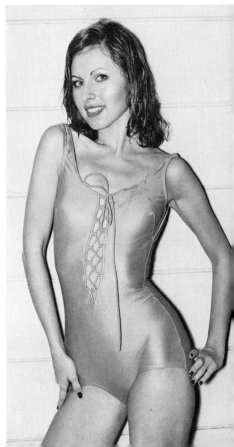

it is possible that it could hit the lens unless a go-bo is placed between it and the lens.

The photographer with a low ceiling should consider the use of the Soff Box on a freewheeling light stand.

In my second studio, which is smaller than my number one, I find this system works well. An 800-watt power pack at the base of the stand gives stability to the topheavy weight of the Soff Box.

Another strobe-contained system which I use when not in the studio is a type of portable strobe called the Larson Starfish. This is similar to the Soff Box but is in the round hex shape rather than square. The advantage of the Starfish is its easy portability.

The Strobosol is connected to the Starfish, making a single unit of diffuser, lamp head and power pack. The stand, Starfish and strobe unit can be transported by car to any location. When I am working in my own home, I use the Starfish in bedrooms and other parts of the house.

So here you have my three types of soft lighting: the 6-foot hex for the larger studio, the square Soff Box for the smaller studio and the portable Starfish for working around the house.

I rarely use hard lighting on glamour subjects except under unusual circumstances. For example, a spotlight might be used for multiple-exposure shots where I am photographing a model against a black background and wish to concentrate the light in only one place. Then there are the mood pictures where I want to have an overall dark effect and light only specific areas of the picture such as parts of the body. The face, the torso, the legs might each be lit separately, bringing lights in from the most flattering angles. This is not possible with

Creating a room setting in a studio environment by hanging lace curtains against background and directing light onto the background so that slight diffused effect results. Light on model is from above camera directly on center. Hair light from top left. Model, Melissa Prophet. Bounce Indoor Diagram 9

bounce light because it is too broad. Several small spot-lights will accomplish the job.

Recently I was attempting to create a moody, romantic illustration for my daughter's latest poetry book. The models, a young man and woman, sat at a table set with silverware, wineglasses and candles. Bounce light just would not work. The flat soft light would have completely overpowered the weak candle. I looked around the studio for some small spotlights and all were too strong—from 150 to 1000 watts. Finally I went into the kitchen where we store extra bulbs for the house and brought back two 75-watt reflector spot bulbs. One was placed behind the man and the other behind the woman. Each was di-rected toward the opposite person. The balance between the spots and the candle was perfect—neither too strong nor too weak.

Intensity can be diminished by turning the lights slightly off the subject so that only the edge of the beam is used. Intensity can also be controlled by moving the lights in closer or pushing them farther back.

Main light is placed to left of camera giving cross-lighting to bosom area and shadowing part of face. Model, Dawn Hanzlik. Bounce Indoor Diagram 9

Postery-type lighting achieved by using a 72-inch Larson Hex with 800-watt Norman strobe from behind camera and four Strobasols illuminating background (two on each side). Shadows are eliminated from background and dark edges outline body contours. Model, Jennie Neumann. Bounce Indoor Diagram 9

Main light placed to right of camera
emphasizes shimmery dress and places
one side of face in shadow. Not all features
can take this type of lighting. Study facial
contours and effects of light placement first.
Four Strobasols on background eliminate
shadows. Model, Dawn Hanzlik. Bounce
Indoor Diagram 9

Model Linda Horn posing between chrome bars can change mood of picture just by her expression and hair style. Main light was placed slightly to right and above camera, thus practically eliminating shadows on face. Orange background was substituted for white in photograph with curly hair. Bounce Indoor Diagrams 8 and (at right) 9

The postery effect by placing light slightly to left of camera gives shadow area to bosoms and emphasizes the body contours. Care was taken to see that Diane Zapanta's arm did not shadow her face completely. Bounce Indoor Diagram 11

Another use of a hard spotlight was a picture of Brooke Mills. I wanted edge light on her face. A 1000-watt quartz light was placed directly behind her face and toward the camera so that her head blocked the lamp from hitting the lens. The skin and fine hairs on her cheek picked up the light so that it rimmed her face. I also tried a drop of water on her finger and used a Kordel Star Filter to create a burst of light at that point. Then we replaced the drop of water with a diamond ring for even more sparkle.

You may wonder why the 1000-watt quartz lamp did not cook her skin. We used a dimmer so that the light was cut down to only a fraction of its power. Why choose a 1000-watt light if we plan to use less? Because I want the capability of more power when using this as a bounce system. Bouncing a light against a surface and then onto the subject naturally decreases the amount of light that

Teresa Parker's dark hair needs the hair light and backlights to keep it from blending into the background. Compact pose features her curvy legs and provocative smile. Bounce Indoor Diagram 12

Cowgirl Tina Hedgren with main light placed slightly to right of camera and four Strobasols on background. Bounce Indoor Diagram 8

hits the subject, so it is necessary under those conditions to have greater power. A word of warning—color changes take place when the Kelvin is lowered. A 1000-watt lamp at full power will give normal color with tungsten film but if the power is lowered the picture takes on an orange cast.

Another technique that I prefer is using a minimum of front light on the subject. In fact, I usually use only one. The broad source created by the 72-inch Hex, the 42-inch Soff Box and the 52-inch Starfish gives a roundness to the full-length figure. I want to emphasize that it is important to use a broad source in order to be most flattering.

When moving in for a close-up I will, on occasion, use a second light. Here I want to keep the shadows very soft or eliminate them entirely. There is more about portrait lighting in the preceding chapter.

Backlighting is something that I firmly approve of. I use five on most of my backlit studies. I love the dramatic effect of a model photographed against a black background with an edge light around her entire body.

Photographing clothes with dark printed fabric requires bounce light to eliminate shadows and to show off the pattern. Dancing figures were pasted onto white studio wall. Bounce Indoor Diagram 9 (reverse key)

Black backgrounds are extremely flattering provided there is ample backlighting so that the model stands out. Main light here in this picture of Kathy McCullen is directly on camera (slightly above since it is a 72-inch Hex) and two backlights on either side of model are directed toward her body. Go-bo's are needed to protect lights from hitting lens. Bounce Indoor Diagram 12 (reverse key)

Actress-model Karen Stride has beautiful long chestnut hair which would be lost to the black background if it were not for the hair lights and four backlights directed toward her from behind. Bounce Indoor Diagram 12 (reverse key)

To give action in these pictures of Karen Stride a motor from portable Jacuzzi was improvised as "fan." Plenty of backlighting adds to the windblown look. Bounce Indoor Diagram 12 (reverse key)

For advertising accounts the photographer must be able to improvise settings and costumes, as here with Jennie Neumann in harem scene. Bounce Indoor Diagram 12 (reverse key)

Generally I place two backlights on each side, protected from hitting the lens by two screens. I use a hair light from a high angle.

Backlighting is best with a dark background but it can have a different effect when used with a light background. The lighter the background the more washed-out the edge lighting on the figure or portrait. Used in conjunction with star filters and light, frilly clothing, such lighting can produce some poetic illustrations.

In using backlights it is important to be cautious about the lights hitting the model's face if she turns her head slightly. The body may look fine but the features are distorted by the bright highlights. This can be avoided by the use of additional small go-bo's. Sometimes I use a magazine or a piece of cardboard to screen the light away from a small area of the picture such as the face.

Arm hiding waistline of Gayna Reed is not a flattering position; however, the candid pose with beret has an impish quality. Hasselblad. Bounce Indoor Diagram 1 (reverse key)

The calendar nude is more salable when the model is featured with simple props and plain background. Gowlandflex 4 x 5. Bounce Indoor Diagram 12

Alice Gowland puts finishing touches on toenails of model Stephanie McLean.

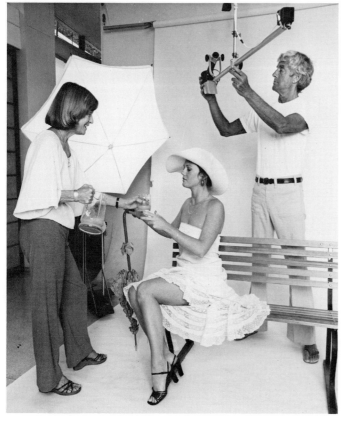

It is important that model's comfort be considered. Here, Alice offers Alex Danforth some orange juice.

Model Karen Maybay with mustache of milk has features that tolerate the side lighting created by the Larson Hex placed slightly to camera right. Bounce Indoor Diagram 9

Candid photograph of Gayna Reed made during nude session. Hasselblad. Bounce Indoor Diagram 12 (reverse key)

*Backlighting with use of black background
creates a white edge light to hair and body.
Flat front light is flattering to facial features.
Actress, Anja Brown. Bounce Indoor
Diagram 12*

THE MODEL

THE
CLASSIC
NUDE—
CONTROLLED
LIGHT

Finding a model who fits all of my requirements for figure photography is most difficult. The Puritan ethic is still with us, and while many individuals accept nudity as a normal part of life, there is still enough of a stigma attached to unclothed humans that many girls shy away from posing, even though the pictures are artistic rather than erotic.

People are surprised to hear me say that I have trouble finding good figure models. Somehow the supposition is

Use of slim-line prop assists model in developing her pose. Pentax, terrazzo floor with curved background. Direct Indoor Diagram 5

that a photographer based in Hollywood can pick and choose any girl. Not so. While legal restrictions have relaxed, the girls who are exceptionally pretty in face and figure and who are amenable to posing nude are snapped up by the men's magazines and paid unrealistically huge sums of money. Thereafter they are not interested in posing for artistic nudes or semi-nudes unless they receive equal compensation. That puts most photographers out of the nude business.

Because I am established as a photographer I am constantly interviewing girls from modeling agencies, sent to me by friends, and others who have read my books or seen my work. This means that I have a steady flow of possibilities for glamour modeling. The majority do not want to pose nude. Once in a while I find a girl who is artistically inclined, who would not want to appear in a men's magazine but who would not be opposed to the classic nude. In the majority of cases these girls are dancers. Somehow the two subjects go together. On these rare occasions I am quick to make a definite appointment, before the girl changes her mind.

I look for a girl with a trim, well-proportioned figure. The height is not as important as the proportions. While many artists prefer the heavier, rounder, more fleshy subjects, I want to emphasize smooth contours, well-defined body structure. Perhaps that is why the dancers so often fit the image. They also have an ability to pose, to fall into graceful positions automatically. They are not merely interested in the financial outcome but in creating something of lasting beauty.

LIGHTING

When I'm asked to critique the work of aspiring photographers I find the one drawback to most work, particularly with figure studies, is the inability to *see* the lighting. Shadows will be crisscrossing the face and body in unflattering patterns, and the photographer is oblivious to the reason the pictures are disappointing. This is why I always suggest that one work with a single light source at first, moving it and observing carefully what effect it has on the subject. Shadows are subtle to the naked eye. Most people don't even notice them. But to the camera they can be definite and harsh.

A common denominator to most of my studio pictures where I have control of the lighting is the shadowless backgrounds. I like the figure to stand out with no interference by shadows that it might cast. I use as many as four lights on the background and sometimes none on the model!

The type of light is not important except that with strobe one is not able to determine exactly what the result will be unless the pilot light is very strong. With the use of

Dancer seated on dry terrazzo floor with background lighted and no lights on model. Slight "spill" gives edge highlights to facial features. Pentax, Plus X film developed in D76, 1 to 1. Direct Indoor Diagram 5

flood or quartz lights one has the advantage of knowing immediately what effect the placement has on both the figure and background.

The use of four lights on the background (two from each side) produces a silhouette effect, and I found quite by accident one evening that by pouring a small amount of water on my studio floor, which is made of terrazzo, the model's silhouette was repeated. The variety of poses and effects was countless. My model, a slim girl of only ninety-eight pounds, was also a dancer. Later on I moved the lights gradually so that they illuminated part of her figure. This brought about an entirely different set of pictures. I've since used this same technique with other girls, and in each case the individual figure and personality brought a different aspect to the pictures.

By varying the direction of the lights on the background and aiming them slightly toward the model, another possibility presents itself. The body is partially lit. If more detail is desired I will place a broad source of light either directly over the camera or on either side, depending on the effect it has.

The lights used on the background need not be large. They can be spots or quartz or stobe. However, when lights are used on the model they should be from a wide source. Usually a bounce light is good. I may use a 36-inch Larson Reflectasol and bounce the quartz light off of that, or I will use my strobe and bounce if off of the reflector, or I will use the Soff Box. This is a 36-inch-square reflected surface where the light is encased inside, producing a soft effect rather than harsh shadows.

I can remember very clearly when photographing my first nude model I had only two photoflood lights with simple aluminum reflectors. Rather than use them both to light the model, I placed one on the backgrond and used the other at different angles, watching to see how the various positions changed the shadow patterns. My preference was established at that time as I noticed that less light on the figure made it more flattering and interesting.

When adding the dimension of water to nude studies under controlled lighting conditions, one never knows what the result will be. One prop I built was a shallow tub (details in Chapter 12) that would contain water. Using two different methods of lighting produced two com-

The ideal nude model has lovely facial features, graceful hands, a smooth skin and sensitivity to the mood desired. Bounce Indoor Diagram 14 (reverse light), plus hair light

Silhouette produced by use of background lights only. Floor reflection is caused by water poured on terrazzo. Direct Indoor Diagram 5

Dramatic shadows on the female figure are the result of using a hard, direct light emanating from camera right slightly behind model. A second light is directed against background from camera left. Direct Indoor Diagram 6

Late-afternoon sun, around the pool, provides a nice edge light to the face of Linda Horn. A gold reflector emphasized the warmth of the sun at that late hour. 240mm lens on Gowlandflex 4 x 5. Daylight Diagram 5

The soft light of shaded area with use of Reflectasol to illuminate the face of model Susan Hill is propitious to the setting. Picture was taken in public rose garden but low angle eliminates unsightly background. Daylight Diagram 5

This picture of Kathy McCullen combines the elements important for a successful beach pin-up: ideal California girl, close cropping, low angle for colorful sky, motion of water, backlighting for the hair and a perfect exposure, taken on a 4 x 5 transparency for easier sale! Gowlandflex 4 x 5, hand-held. Daylight Diagram 6

Soft, outdoor portrait of Karen Maybay is made by use of a gold reflector, which is extremely flattering to skin. Most models cannot look into the bright glare without frowning. Daylight Diagram 5

Popular as stock photographs are poses of girls against plain backgrounds. Here a board was extended into the picture so that Kathy Morrison would have something to lean on. Bounce Indoor Diagram 9 (reverse key)

Same model, same backlighting, but this time an electronic flash unit (Norman 200-B) is used as a key light. While the skin is not as warm-toned, a less strained expression results. Hasselblad 150mm lens. Daylight Diagram 6

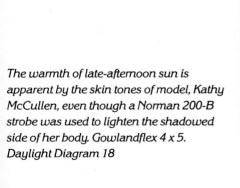

The warmth of late-afternoon sun is apparent by the skin tones of model, Kathy McCullen, even though a Norman 200-B strobe was used to lighten the shadowed side of her body. Gowlandflex 4 x 5. Daylight Diagram 18

Finding outdoor locations for nude photography is not easy. Here the back garden of a friend's home, dried from the summer sun, makes a bright area against which to place the model's figure. Daylight Diagram 5

A gold reflector is used to bounce the sun onto this backlit study of Jean Manson in front of Gowland home. Gowlandflex 4 x 5. Daylight Diagram 5

In order to have a soft lighting effect I built this room setting in my front driveway and placed a sheet over the top where the sun was diffused. Daylight Diagram 16

Compact torso study of Roxanne Katon taken with the Gowlandflex 4 x 5, Norman 200-B strobe, and Daylight 120 Ektachrome. Daylight Diagram 6

Using the sun to outline the figure, model is seated, letting the water create a reflective pattern and keeping her body almost in silhouette. Daylight Diagram 3

During school hours we can photograph in our stream which runs year-round. With the model against the clear area, her body is backlit and stands out in an otherwise sylvan setting. Daylight Diagram 5

In order to have a clear area and separate the model from the background, our 5 x 7 Gowlandflex was raised to shoot down against the blue water of the pool, which also gives complimentary color for the skin tones. Daylight Diagram 6

Many foreign markets do not permit the showing of pubic hair, so one must find natural poses to conceal the area without being obvious. Bounce Indoor Diagram 4

On a partly cloudy day with the sun going in and out, the clouds were reflected in the man-made lake, and a touch of sparkle from partial rays of the sun made this picture especially moody and appealing. Overcast day

pletely distinctive pictures. In one we used a black background and turned the lights toward the model rather than toward the background, and this gave the water a reflective surface as well as a crystal-like effect when the water was in motion. For the other picture we used the same tub but left the background white, and turned all four lights on the background. These were strobe lights, and when the water was poured the motion was stopped. The proximity of the model to the background caused enough reflected light to hit her body so that detail was discernible. Although the water is only 4 inches deep the black plastic base gives it the appearance of greater depth.

Another experiment in lighting was a box that I built containing two strobe lights, one at the bottom and one almost centered. The box was about 8 feet square. I stretched a sheet over one side and the back was placed against the wall. I wanted to see the effect of diffused light coming from behind the subject and at both sides. I knew that the area where the light was placed would photograph brighter, and for that reason I tried to pose the model so that her head would cover the center strobe and her buttocks the one at the bottom. The areas where the lights were placed did tend to wash out her image, so

Dancer Iris Rounsaville is caught in the graceful transition from one movement to another by use of Pentax camera, Plus X film. Direct Indoor Diagram 5

I decided to use only half of the box and put a black background over the other half. When I wanted color in the picture, I substituted a color background for the black.

You might want to try using a grainy effect. I did this for an assignment for Berkey Colortran lighting. Eastman Kodak recording film with an ASA rating of 1000 will give more grain. My negatives seemed thin and underexposed, so I decided to intensify them by using Kodak Chromium Intensifier. It's a simple operation conducted with lights on. The negative is first soaked for ten minutes (if it has been dried previously), then put into the intensifier for three to five minutes until the black image is bleached yellow. Then it is washed in clear water and then put into the clearing bath provided with the intensifier, until it returns to nearly white (about two minutes).

Side lighting is important to bring out the roundness of the body. A second light was used to light the background and separate the model from the background. Direct Indoor Diagram 6

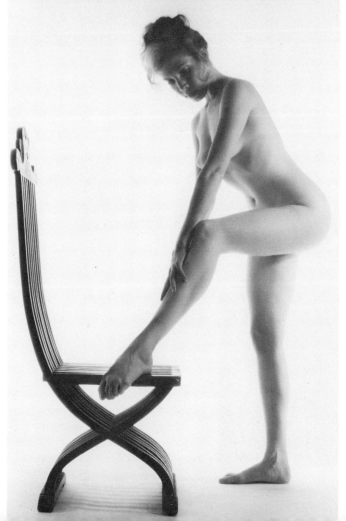

Working with simple props aids the subject in suggesting poses. Use of two lights provides shadows so effective with the nude figure. Bounce Indoor Diagram 14

After rewashing it is then redeveloped in a paper de-
veloper D-72 until the white image is blackened completely. Then it is washed and dried. The result was more
than I had anticipated. The grain of the negative had
increased! Now there was grain even in the shadow
areas. (You may want to try even a simpler method. With
a normal negative use a screen over the paper when
printing. These screens available through Director Enterprises, 1926 S. Pacific Coast Highway, Suite 232, Re-
dondo Beach, CA 90277. The company has charcoal-,
line-etch and white-etch varieties.)

The entire sitting involved only two lights: the key light
was a 36-inch super-silver Larson Reflectasol reflecting a
1000-watt quartz light. This was used to light the body.
The second light was the 600-watt quartz which was
used to light the background on the opposite side of the
other light. I found that when the body is lighted against a
wall, the side of the body which is getting the main source
is light and the other side is dark. Here was a case where I
didn't want the entire background lighted, but only half,

*The simple use of daylight coming through
a curtained window produces the
cross-lighting most effective in figure
configuration. Daylight Diagram 15*

Use of a dark background enhances the intimacy when the body is edge-lighted from both sides. Direct Indoor Diagram 7

so that the dark part of her body had a white background and the light part of her body was against a dark background. I was able to split the background by use of a go-bo in front of the 600-watt quartz.

As a change from the plain studio background, I like to use home settings. I prefer those offering something either of old-world charm or ultramodern furnishings.

With the abundance of wooden floors, walls and ceilings one needs controlled lighting. The dark surfaces require a greater amount of exposure than does the subject. With the use of strobe it would be difficult to see exactly what the light is doing. Polaroids help, but each time the subject changes position the lighting could drastically change the shadowed effect. In the home situation I prefer the use of quartz or flood lights. Two lights are sufficient, but a third to be used as a hair light is advantageous.

I like to keep the mood of the girl in tune with the surroundings. So if the furniture suggests past eras I look for compatible touches of clothing and hair style.

The indoor settings require the use of tungsten film. However, when one is working near a window the daylight brings a bluish cast to that portion of the body or prop where the light strikes. Sometimes this is flattering

Straight lines of antique chair make pleasing contrast to the contours of subject's body as brought out by the side lighting. Direct Indoor Diagram 6

I designed and built this combination of two boxes which separate and can be used individually or together. Boxes are lined with foil and house two strobe heads and two floods in each. Power pack is below in covered base. Home designed "body light"

and other times one would want to balance the color with that of the indoor lighting. There are two ways to do this. First, if you are using tungsten film a sheet of orange plastic placed over the window, on the outside where it will not be obvious, would bring the red tones needed to warm the blue of daylight. One could also switch to daylight film and use blue filters over the lights, or blue bulbs that have been corrected for daylight. Light equipped with a dimmer enables control of the contrast.

There is still a good market for the classic calendar nude. The pictures differ from those already covered in that the girl is generally looking into the camera with either a smile or a provocative look, and her body is lighted to show detail with only slight shadows. The importance of selectivity in choosing a model is even greater here then for strictly artistic photos. To sell calendar nudes one must find a girl with flawless skin, beautiful breasts, well-formed torso and legs, beautiful facial features and shiny hair. Not an easy task.

Using available light from window only, the side light gives nice shadow contours to the nude figure. Daylight Diagram 10 (indoors)

In this photograph only the one key light was used to give definite hard shadows. Key was the same as in Direct Indoor Diagram 15

This market still requires that no pubic hair be show-ing, and for variety some small piece of clothing can be evident. The key word is simplicity. A calendar must be designed so that it catches the eye, so the less jumble with furniture or scarves or props the better. Blue backgrounds and black backgrounds are the most popular because they seem to enhance the skin tones.

Calendar markets prefer a 4 x 5 format or larger. If the picture is exceptional they will take a 2¼ x 2¼. Trans-parencies rather than color negatives are required.

Changing of pose requires replacement of the light. If strobes had been used one could not see what effect the light would be having. Some strobes do have strong pilot lights that would help, but in using the floods one knows for sure in advance just what the shadow pattern will be. Second light not used in these poses. Direct Indoor Diagram 15

A diffusion screen of spun glass over 1000-watt light softens the shadows. Second fill light was not used. Direct Indoor Diagram 15

Same picture with use of a diffusion filter over the lens to create a soft, misty effect. Second light not used. Direct Indoor Diagram 15

Limberness of Gayna Reed creates an interesting form in this candid picture. Direct Indoor Diagram 6

Dramatic dance pose using hair movement at moment of exposure gives a candid quality to a pre-posed study. Direct Indoor Diagram 6

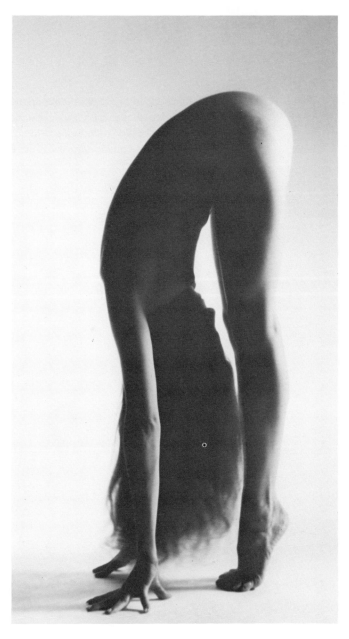

Girls who are extremely limber such as dancer Linda York have the ability to assume unconventional poses, which look like sculpture when lighted in this manner. Direct Indoor Diagram 6

Reflections from water on floor created interesting shapes with figure of dancer. These were taken with Fujinon lens (180mm) on Gowlandflex 4 x 5. Direct Indoor Diagram 5

9

FASHION

When I think of fashion photography the editorial pictures in *Vogue, Bazaar* and *Elle* all come to mind as the ultimate in this form of photography. In this arena the world's most creative photographers have a chance to show their talents. Only a chosen few ever become staff photographers for leading high-style magazines, but seeing their work is an inspiration to all glamour photographers. Many of the techniques they use can be imitated and adapted for other markets. Looking at the genius of Richard Avedon, whose imaginative energy in the photography of women and fashion seems to have no limit, one can see that it is not merely technique that contributes to success in this medium, but an entire personality and individual drive.

The advertisements in these choice magazines also show a greater trend toward imaginative and daring presentation than do the general women's magazines. Nudity, for example, is displayed frequently, but always with a high degree of taste. Ads for skin care, figure control and relaxation techniques use partial or full nudes. In this area, the advertisers use the photographer of their choice rather than a staff person, so the field is open to all.

Then there is the broader marketplace, the general women's magazines, the teen fashions, the clothing catalogs and local advertisers. The ready-to-wear field has grown so rapidly in the last twenty years that there is enough photography to go around.

I have done a limited amount of actual fashion work, where I was hired to photograph the clothing and not the model, mainly for lingerie or sports clothes for local advertisers. I probably could have done more if I had wanted to court the various clients, but frankly I prefer concentrating on the girl rather than the clothing. I like to photograph fashion models, using my own ideas and with no interference by admen or agency art directors. Usually the pictures end up as portfolio material or for my own books. Working with garments involves teams of people, stylists, hairdressers, makeup personnel, coordinators, and others. There are racks of clothing, accessories, props. This is a field where one cannot work alone with the model on a one-to-one basis. So for those of you who are dedicated to becoming fashion photographers, be prepared for a group effort.

A black seamless paper with Christmas lights poked through at varying intervals creates a star effect by using a Kordel star filter for this black-on-black fashion study. Bounce Indoor Diagram 6

Too many beginners in photography think that owning a 35mm outfit and being expert at using it qualifies them for any type of photographic job. Not so. In the commercial world one must also know how to work with larger film formats and with various types of lighting other than available light and how to work with people individually and in groups. The 35mm cameras are used extensively in the fashion world but mainly editorially. The manufacturer who is lucky enough to have his line of clothing selected for an editorial spread is happy with the candid quality of 35mm when models are sent on exotic locations. But when he is paying thousands of dollars for an advertisement in the same magazine he wants his garments to appear clear, sharp, free of unsightly wrinkles and lighted to perfection. Because retouching may be involved in the final picture, the larger negatives are preferable both in color and in black and white.

Clearly many types of fashion markets emerge: the high-fashion editorial, the general women's editorial, catalogs, newspaper ads and individual advertisements for various publications.

Editorial layouts permit the photographer the utmost in creative freedom, but it is possible to combine an individual ad with an editorial sitting. Once a particular idea for a setting is decided on, variations in lighting and posing can slant the pictures in a particular direction. A typical example is the ad done for the fur vest. The advertiser wanted the feeling of night, so we used black on black. Christmas lights were pushed through the paper background and a long lens with a star filter gave them just the hint of sparkle needed to carry out the night effect. Daylight from a side window was supplemented by a 600-watt quartz light bounced from a silver reflector on the other side. When we finished with this series we removed the lights, leaving holes in the background, then tore a large hole in the center of the paper—an old trick—to show a new line of lingerie. The model was able to work in and around this opening. Two types of lighting were used. When she walked through our Norman

Black paper roll in front of a white wall with Christmas lights poked through at intervals and an irregular opening for the model to walk through is lighted by a single Larson 72-inch Hex from the front and two lights on the white background. Model, Sharon Carlson. Bounce Indoor Diagram 8

Pamela La Grande is an ideal fashion model because she has a slim figure and exuberant personality with an ability to twist her body. Bounce Indoor Diagram 8 (reverse key)

Working with two models presents an interesting challenge to the photographer. Pamela La Grande and Kathy Clark had not met before posing but worked well together. Direct Indoor Diagram 14

By placing the strobe tube directly next to the lens by means of an aluminum box constructed for that purpose, a flat light is cast onto the subjects, reaching under the visor and chin and casting minimal shadow on background. Direct Indoor Diagram 1

Models are placed away from the background with the background lighted separately and one hard light on the camera. Bottom of print was darkened in printing. Direct Indoor Diagram 14

A single window to right of camera furnishes the total illumination and makes interesting shadows on the body. Model, Sharon Carlson. Daylight Diagram 13

strobe bounced against our 72-inch Hex lighted her from directly front. The white background seen through the hole was lighted by the use of four Strobasols (two on each side). Finally, we used daylight only. It came through the use of sunlight from a side window of diffused glass. This lit the background and one side of the model's body. Exposure was 1/60 at f/5.6.

In contrast to this situation is the use of a plain white background. Here one can use props, or work with paper rolls or mirrors or use the background alone. A trend in European fashion pictures is to use one hard light next to the camera, throwing shadows on the background, something that we tried to avoid when learning the A B C's of correct techniques. But the fashion world is constantly changing styles, so pictures must change accordingly even if they break rules! I like to wash out shadows when using a white background, so I place my

After we have worked out technical requirements for the use of flash and establishing a focus and flash distance point, the model is asked to "walk through" that distance so that the shutter is fired at the instant she reaches the size on the groundglass. An area with minimum amount of background distraction was previously selected. Model, Stephanie McLean. Hasselblad. Daylight Diagram 6

models far enough away from the wall to enable the two Strobasols to hit the background and overpower the shadows cast by the side or front lights. At other times when working with the models directly against a wall I use a homemade ring light. This is a unit that surrounds my lens, thus the light comes from all sides and barely a shadow is distinguishable. Another advantage to the ring light is that it helps to soften wrinkles in skin and fabric. Ring lights are also available commercially.

Newspaper ads require working with groups of models and several garments for each girl or boy. The backgrounds are plain and the lighting basically from front rather than harsh side light. The photographer must work with professional models who know how to change a hair style quickly or add an accessory and who have the stamina and enthusiasm to don from ten to fifteen garments at a sitting. Very similar to this is catalog

Extreme flat light obtained by placing the strobe tube directly above the lens by means of the aluminum box constructed for that purpose. Model, Stephanie McLean. Direct Indoor Diagram 1

These three pictures illustrate the technique of moving back from the model once a pose has been established. Camera and flash remained at the same distance but telephoto 150mm lens was used for the two close-ups. An 80mm was used for the full-length. Model, Stephanie McLean. Daylight Diagram 6

To illustrate extreme makeup, Andrea Blahd in plumed hat and choker is photographed inside a church, next to a window.

work, where hundreds of garments are photographed in single day. The 2¼ format is used extensively in such work. If the pictures are to be taken in a studio, preparations are made days ahead with the rental of props, hiring of stylists, hairdressers, etc. Photographers who gain catalog contracts are skilled technicians who can work fast.

Some of the better catalog work is done on location. In outdoor settings one must look for complimentary or plain backgrounds. I generally use my Norman 200 portable strobe unit with backlighting whenever possible. All garments are pressed and hung on a clothes rack which we transport in a rented van. We look for locations with a variety of backgrounds to avoid frequent change of locale.

What type of girl is the fashion model? Times have changed since the 1950s, when fashion models were mainly of two types: the high-fashion girl, who had a very gaunt and mature look, and the typical young college-age girl. Today models have become more realistic. The girls in *Vogue* and *Bazaar* have taken on the young, sexy look rather than the gaunt, unfriendly appearance of the '50s. The all-American look is still in but the girls are younger and younger, some even as young as thirteen modeling adult clothing. The fashion girl is still taller than the commercial model. She must be at least 5 feet 7 inches and preferably taller. Her weight at 5 feet 7 should be no more than 115. Most popular of all is the California-girl look. She's a blond, tan, slender but not skinny. Girls with large bosoms just don't work out well as fashion models, although today's fashion girl is a bit more chesty than her earlier counterpart, who had practically no bosom.

Those who want to follow a career as a fashion model must learn how to apply makeup in a variety of ways and arrange their hair in different styles, and do it all quickly. They must have a flair for clothing and maintain a simple but diversified wardrobe, even though most of the jobs will be in the clothing of some manufacturer. The fashion model must know how to move, to feel comfortable in front of the camera, and to work well and closely with other models even though they have never met before. She must also have physical stamina, for it takes energy to change clothes quickly and often during a sitting. The fashion photographer has the double chore of seeing that both model and clothing are at their best, whereas the glamour photographer can concentrate completely on his model and let the clothes be more casual.

In photographing lingerie, lace curtains hung on a pole in the studio make an appropriate background and help the model in posing. Model, Elizabeth Halsey. Bounce Indoor Diagram 9

*In the middle of a busy street we were able
to find this lot covered with wild mustard.
By climbing on top of the car, we achieved
a high angle that blocked out city traffic.
Casual outfit by designer Jo Lathwood.
Daylight Diagram 2 (reverse sun)*

Colorful Mexican dress by designer Jo Lathwood is photographed against brilliantly painted panels on the Santa Monica pier. Model Annette Molen brings her special personality to add joie de vivre. Daylight Diagram 2

Jennifer Loomis in white kimono with use of side light to bring out folds in white silk fabric. Bounce Indoor Diagram 17

A single light on the camera keeps shadows on the background to a minimum. Model, Kathy Clark. Direct Indoor Diagram 1

Motion, whether it is dramatic or subtle, brings a new dimension to any picture. The photographer is never sure of the result until the film is developed, which makes action pictures more difficult but also more interesting.

Some girls have a natural ability to move gracefully, while others are awkward. I try to work the girl to her own capacity rather than forcing something that does not work. So if I am interested in dramatic action with leaps and turns I will look for a dancer. Dancers are excellent models even when not in action because they have a built-in grace for posing which makes it easier on the photographer.

10
THE
MODEL
IN MOTION

DRAMATIC ACTION

If I am working outdoors, I look for a location that provides a clear background, such as a stretch of beach or a hilltop. To give a feeling of added height when photographing a leap, I will shoot from a low angle, eliminating the ground, so that the girl is suspended in midair. I like to use fast shutter speeds of 1/400, 1/500 and 1/1000 second to freeze the action, but it is possible through rehearsing with the model to catch the peak of the action using a slower shutter speed such as 1/60 or 1/125. The "peak" is the point of movement when the direction is changed from up to down. One has to anticipate the peak, and that takes practice. Film is something I never skimp on when doing action pictures, and I generally go over the same movement for at least one roll (twelve exposures) and then move on to a different pose. The number of exposures depends on the model and her stamina in doing the same thing over and over. A typical example would be the model in the shallow end of a swimming pool, leaping up with arms moving upward at the same time, bringing sprays of water with her. Invariably there will be one exposure that surpasses all the others even though two dozen pictures might have been taken. Water gets in her eyes and mouth each time she emerges. And jumping out of water requires more energy than a leap from the ground, so a girl who is healthy and used to activity makes the best subject.

Dramatic action is possible with the model standing still with the ocean waves providing the movement. Here

An excellent action prop is a bicycle. Model first takes the position for focus and flash distance to balance with the background. Then she backs up and rides into the same spot. Model, Kerry Foutray. Daylight Diagram 6

again one must make many exposures, for quite frequently the force of the water can knock the subject over
or leave her with an amazed or frightened facial expression. This is what I call planned dramatic action. We
position the model so that her body is posed gracefully
either on her knees or seated in the surf, then wait for the
waves to hit!

Dance sequences taken in the studio are easier on the
photographer but not on the model. Our studio has
terrazzo floors, which do not give when the model's feet
hit. I've avoided using a paper roll because the model
might slip. The studio wall is curved both at top and
bottom so that no seams show and the dancer looks as
though she is suspended in air just as at the beach when
shooting from a low angle.

I like to use at least four background lights, to eliminate

*Figure is posed first to feature small waist
and cover bosom—brushing is a
last-minute business before tripping the
shutter. Bounce Indoor Diagram 5*

*Annette Molen, seated in a pile of sawdust
in a local stable, creates her own action by
a spur-of-the-moment gesture. Overcast
day*

shadows on the background,and one key light. The key can be changed with the action. I like the five-light system because it gives a postery effect to the poses.

From past experience I've found it wise when I interview a girl to have her do a little dance sequence to music. In that way I am assured of her ability. The girls who study classic ballet have standard routines which they can run through, selecting only those steps which lend themselves gracefully to pictures. Modern jazz dancers' body movements differ from those of classic ballet, and these unconventional steps combined with an unusual costume can produce striking results.

SUBTLE ACTION

To give pictures a candid look I generally seek a small bit of "business," to use a theatrical term, for the model to do. Here again, the action should be done several times to appear natural and unposed. Just the flip of her hair, or the placing of her hand to her head, or turning to look over her shoulder bring a looser, more casual look to an otherwise stiff pose.

The use of movement in the background either by other people or objects is another way of bringing action into the scene. Moving traffic, birds in flight, people walking become blurred while the model stands still. The amount of blur will depend on the shutter speed. If the desire is an unidentified blur then slow shutter speeds of 1/10 to ½ second will do the trick. Be sure to use a tripod or brace your camera against a firm object with these slow speeds.

Posed action can be effective if your model is graceful. In dancing this would be deciding on a particular step and holding it for the fraction of time the lights are fired. Strobes are best to catch this. Working with couples, I use a form of posed action where one party stands still and the other makes the movement, all decided beforehand. And, of course, I take many exposures to assure a good one. Invariably, in action, the girl's hair will cover her face, or one foot will look awkward, so it takes many tries.

Rehearsed action in studio setup. Body is first posed at a twisted angle and head is spun around at the last minute. Model, Debbie Feuer. Bounce Indoor Diagram 12

Rehearsed action jump by Joan Goulet against a wall of ivy which goes black in the afternoon shade. Backlighting of the sun emphasizes the sparkle of the water and edge-lights her hair and body. Hasselblad 150mm at 1/500. Daylight Diagram 6

Another form of rehearsed action shows dancer Cindi Cook running into prefocused area for a pleasing picture of beach action. Taken on an overcast California day. Daylight Diagram 6

CROSS-CAMERA ACTION

Running pictures are the most difficult in that the cross action of the legs is unpredictable, resulting in unflattering shapes. This is particularly noticeable when the model is running toward the camera. If the subject runs parallel to the background a faster shutter speed is necessary. In both cases a prefocus is established at the point where the picture is to be taken. Then the model backs up and runs through the action. For the cross-camera picture the photographer pans with the running and shoots when he feels it looks good. With the model running toward the photographer, the camera remains still until she reaches the point of focus. Everything is done very quickly and only after the film is developed can one be positive of having captured the most graceful moment.

Black backgrounds with the use of
backlights, in this case four, make a brilliant
commercial picture. Here, Brooke Mills's red
hair is lit by an additional hair light.
Gowlandflex 4 x 5. Bounce Indoor
Diagram 12

Edge lighting with five lights coming from
the back is more effective with a dark
background. Bounce Indoor Diagram 12

One of my favorite lightings—lots of backlight. Even though model Debbie Feuer is wearing black she is outlined by the backlights, making a dramatic picture with impact. Bounce Indoor Diagram 12

A room setting created in a studio gives the photographer more control over his lighting but is still not equal to true boudoir backgrounds because of its limitations in angle, and so forth. Bounce Indoor Diagram 9

Model Teri Groves photographed against a black cloth background. Cloth does not give the shiny effect that sometimes occurs with use of paper backgrounds. 4 x 5 Ektachrome E-6, 210mm lens. Bounce Indoor Diagram 12

Sacramento reservoir and semi-overcast day are the setting for this lovely nude study. Advantage of still water over the ocean is that the reflection is possible. Daylight Diagram 3

One of my favorite combinations—a nude figure and water. Here, created in our studio, is a simple water tub. The backlighting gives sparkle to the splashing water and edge-lights the figure, leaving partial shadows. Bounce Indoor Diagram 12

Use of daylight film with 1000-watt quartz (tungsten) with no blue filter over the light gives an overabundance of orange to the entire picture. Direct Indoor Diagram 15

This is what I call a "nude that is not a nude." Girls who would otherwise not pose nude love this pose. Melissa Prophet is wearing a bikini but it is not evident. Bounce Indoor Diagram 9

With two Mylar mirrors and a black background, a multi-image effect is possible. Changes of hand and arm positions will make a variety of patterns. Bounce Indoor Diagram 17

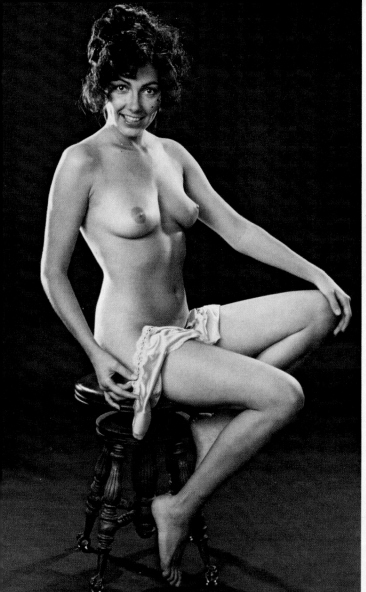

Typical calendar material shows Elizabeth Halsey briefly attired and black background which is excellent for skin tones. Pentax. Bounce Indoor Diagram 12

Stark architectural forms contrast the elegant and chiffony creation worn by model Andrea Blahd. Daylight Diagram 2

Calendar companies like colorful backgrounds that are not cluttered and distracting. Stephanie McLean with bouquet of daisies is posed horizontally to fit technical requirements. Daylight Diagram 6

Using a compact pose to fill the negative, Diane Lienke, who is a tall, athletic model, emphasizes her excellent figure and shapely legs against a clear background. Gowlandflex 4 x 5, hand-held. Daylight Diagram 6

Colorful multiple images created by the use of Mylar mirrors with colorful chiffon thrown over Reflectasols. Model, actress Melonie Haler, has provocative personality and ability to work with interesting costumes and props. Bounce Indoor Diagram 6

Working at a man-made lake, our model assumes an original pose on the plank, thus putting her body in a clear area. Overcast day

Gowland's formula for successful glamour is combined in this 4 x 5 transparency: a healthy, beautiful, California girl, colorful bikini, sparkling water, backlighting with flash key. Model, Stephanie McLean. Gowlandflex 4 x 5. Daylight Diagram 6

With her body turned sideways to the sun's early-morning rays, Susanne Severeid kneels in a pose that emphasizes line and form. Daylight Diagram 1

The early-morning sun casts an orange tone to the body of Susanne Severeid. Daylight Diagram 2

Rehearsal of "peak" action is important in order to anticipate high point. The camera shutter must be pressed just before the model reaches this point because there is a millisecond delay from the time the shutter is fired until the actual picture is made. This is particularly important with single-lens reflex cameras in order to allow time for the reflex mirror to move up before the shutter takes the picture. Model, Anna Neil. Daylight Diagram 3 (reverse sun)

In all three of these photographs the same procedure was followed. First the model was posed, the camera focused and the exposure determined for the distance of the flash and exposure for the background. The f/stop was for the flash and the shutter speed was set according to the background reading. This left only waiting for the wave to break. Get model used to the water first, so that her expression will not be one of surprise! Daylight Diagram 6

A polyurethane rock (opposite), made by Marty Sugarman Enterprises, is of the same material used in making surf boards. It can be moved in and out of the water according to the tide and can be positioned so that the background is clear. Model Marie Cummings had to be careful because of the lightweight properties of the "rock." Its rough exterior scraped her legs when the surf overturned it. Daylight Diagram 6

Slightly blurred effect is possible by having the subject run across the plane of action with a relatively slow shutter speed of 1/125 second. Model, Stephanie McLean. Daylight Diagram 6

Simple action of looking at a small flower gives a candid quality to this study of two girls on a hot summer day. Models, Susan Hill and Rainbow. Overcast day

Action with couples is rehearsed as to picture position, focus is established, and then they are signaled to begin. Models, Camillia Hudson and Tyrone Spears. Daylight Diagram 7

Alison Charie, dancer and actress, first showed several symmetrical positions from her routine, from which these two were selected. Photographer does not have to catch the action, since she is able to hold the pose for the time required. Single light from left keeps body in partial shadow, which is effective in presenting dance forms. Bounce Indoor Diagram 1 (reverse key)

Main light from left and second light on background from the right catches the dramatic leap of dancer Alison Charie. Action was repeated several times. Bounce Indoor Diagram 14

Dancer Tracy Rosenthal rehearses peak action poses from high school musical before caught by camera. Bounce Indoor Diagram 8

The simplest method of shooting action—Pentax with late-afternoon sun. Terry Groves is able to perform unusual stunts while in motion on skates. Daylight Diagram 3 (reverse sun)

Use of strobe with late-afternoon sun almost in back of gymnast Jocelyn Christie makes it possible to capture peak action. Daylight Diagram 7

I consider the beach responsible in part for my becoming involved with the business of glamour photography. Most of my youth was spent on the beaches at Santa Monica where I grew up, and the beach has become an integral part of my life.

With my first camera I chose to photograph some of the teenage girls with whom I associated. Most of these early attempts were pretty sad, but I realize more every day how lucky I was to have had a beginning with a beach location. It is the most natural place in the world to capture the beauty of a woman.

I am of the same opinion today because the beach provides all the elements I look for. The subject is the center of importance but must be backed up by a complimentary background, there must be a spontaneity in her pose, and the setting must have credibility. The beach location offers all three. With the sea or the sand as background the subject stands out. With the movement of water to establish some type of action, a spontaneity is produced, and if she is wearing a bikini, a wet T-shirt or nothing, it is quite believable that with such attire she would be found near the ocean.

Now that I have expounded on the joys of this location, it's only fair to admit some of the frustrations. The main problem is the dependence on weather—conditions are very unpredictable at close proximity to water, causing anxiety in planning a session and sometimes forcing cancellations and postponements. The two most distressing elements are wind and fog.

It is possible, of course, to use both of these to advantage, but it's more comfortable on an ideal day when the wind is at a minimum, the temperature is mild and the skies are clear. Then everything works well: the model is warm and content, eager to please, and doesn't mind getting into the water. The photographer isn't bothered by wind blowing sand into his equipment or salt spray hitting his lens.

The foggy days are good mainly for moody pictures such as those found on album covers or perfume ads or as illustrations for poetic greeting cards. Here the misty atmosphere which almost completely eliminates the sea, leaving only a touch of water, can create dreamlike effects.

During the months from June through August the beaches of California have considerable fog and it is

11

SAND AND SEA

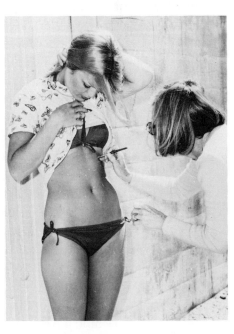

Alice Gowland uses a small brush with light makeup to touch up moles on model's stomach. Later these are blotted and powdered.

161

Peter Gowland turns his Hasselblad upside down to get a high angle with clear sand background on model Joan Geletko. Norman 200-B strobe.

almost impossible to take early-morning photographs (the time of day I most prefer). We can go for weeks with no sun on the coastline, but only a mile away, where my studio is located, the sky will be clear and blue and the sun bright. Can you imagine the exasperation to the professional whose client has requested a snappy picture when day after day goes by with fog or mist? Yes, I must confess that the pressure created by deadlines combined with miserable weather conditions can be most difficult.

When I am faced with the need to work with less than perfect weather conditions, I use two methods. If the sky is only partly overcast I proceed as though it were sunny and use strobe or reflector to balance the shadow side of the model with the bright hazy background. On the heavy, misty morning when there is little hope that the sun will break through, I work toward that misty effect using no fill and letting the model go dark, which results in a somber overall feeling. There are fog filters that are available, and also diffusion filters that will enhance the already foggy picture.

A 4 x 5 Polaroid is taken to make sure of the correct exposure and to help the model pose correctly.

In winter months a plastic bottle filled with hot water is taken to the beach along with other equipment. To give the model a wet look the hot water is used over tank top just before end of shooting.

In taking a backlit portrait around a swimming pool area, assistant Dean Cuadra holds white tabletop improvised as a fill-in reflector.

In order to take spontaneous action Peter Gowland likes to dress informally in bare feet and shorts so that he can easily follow the action without worry of the surf.

I advise using Plus X or Panatomic X film to get more contrast. Verichrome Pan is softer, and better with hard sunlight. In color I use Kodachrome 25 for 35mm cameras and Ektachrome for the larger cameras such as 2¼, 4 x 5 and 5 x 7.

But now let's get to good beach weather—those warm mornings when the wind has not yet arrived, the air is clear, the beaches are free of people, and I have a lovely model ready to be photographed. I've learned to follow a certain procedure in order to make the day go smoother. First, we plan to arrive on the beach around 8:00 A.M., and we do not anticipate working more than three hours. Both model and photographer become bored and tired (and hungry) after that time, the wind comes up, and people begin arriving with their Frisbees and picnic baskets. Secondly, I have a number of assistants. Alice, my wife, is my number one. I call her the director, and she takes care of scheduling, costuming, seeing that the model's hair is freshly washed and that her makeup is neat and not overdone. I have one paid assistant who varies from time to time because my shooting schedule is variable, so I must find someone who needs only a part-time job. I like an assistant who knows as much technically as I do or even more, someone who learns my routine very quickly and can anticipate my needs.

Because I use a variety of cameras I like to have one or two strong young people, interested in photography, who will come along as "gofers." They carry equipment, run back and forth from setting to where our gear is

Working with couples is often more fun than working with a single model. Each helps the other in gaining a more natural pose. Actor Richard Briskin and model Lori Lethin had not worked together before.

This young couple had not modeled before and needed pictures for their portfolio. Water and sunshine and a little direction from the photographer help to create a pleasing situation. Hasselblad camera with Norman strobe fill. Models, Stephanie McLean and Robert Pinkerton. Daylight Diagram 6

stationed and are willing and ready for all types of tasks.

I want to emphasize here that it is only because I use my Pentax 35mm, my Hasselblad and the Gowlandflex interchangeably that I need so many helping hands. If you are using one camera and a minimum of portable props, the fewer people the better. I do believe, however, that any type of glamour work is benefited when the photographer has at least one person to help him, preferably a woman. This leaves him free to concentrate on technical matters.

Another tip in this respect: in screening assistants I try to select someone who will be a "silent" partner. There have been instances when helpers, meaning well, offered advice to the model or to me or took the liberty of moving a prop. This is very irritating. Those who ask many questions are also a drag on the sitting. So no matter whom you select to help you, be sure you have an understanding beforehand about who is in charge!

My paid assistant loads film, gives me meter readings, measures flash distance from camera to model and confers on technical questions. My other assistants will hold the flash.

We carry big beach towels on which to place our equipment, two or three bottles of hot water, one bottle of drinking water, a small ladder and miscellaneous props selected for that particular day. One prop that has proved

Before working in a wet-down situation the models are photographed in casual clothing. Romantic situations such as this lend themselves easily to advertising or editorial layouts. Hasselblad, Norman 200-B strobe and 80mm lens. Daylight Diagram 6 (reverse sun)

With sun at high noon, lighting is best with head tipped back. Here Camillia Hudson and Tyrone Spears form a compact horizontal pose so often requested for billboards and bus ads. Norman 200-B strobe fill. Daylight Diagram 5

Taking nude pictures on public beaches is still a problem, so Karen Stride poses in camisole and briefs that can be removed quickly when beach is private. Daylight Diagram 6

Semi-nude portrait in the surf shows model-actress Karen Stride in serious mood. Flash fill with Hasselblad and Norman strobe give sharp detail to features. Daylight Diagram 6

Using a parasol as a prop, model-actress Karen Stride braces herself against the force of a wave as it hits against her back. Waves add action to an otherwise static picture. Daylight Diagram 6

Joan Geletko in horizontal pose with sun backlighting the figure and darkened area filled in with Norman 200-B strobe. Daylight Diagram 6

Same pose is held while strobe is disconnected, and silhouette effect is the result. Daylight Diagram 3

invaluable is the partial hull of a catamaran that I mentioned finding on the beach. It fits easily into my trunk but takes two people to carry it across the sand.

Before leaving our studio my equipment is completely checked over. I carry a Norman 200 strobe unit and a backup Honeywell 780. The Norman has two heads, and I use one with a 15-foot extension cord. I also carry an extra battery for the Norman. If I were an amateur I would limit my cameras to one format with two lenses, a normal and a semi-tele.

The model has been selected for a particular photo. The beach girl should have a trim figure, not necessarily a full bosom as many may think. She should have no excess fat, looking as though she cares about herself. I prefer beach subjects to have a slight tan. White skin looks somehow naked in a bikini and the flesh never looks as firm. Yet too much tan can pose a problem. Definite tan marks make it impossible to change bikini styles. White lines will show where the cut of the suit is different. Also a girl who has recently acquired a tan, or re-exposed her tan, will have a reddish tint to the skin that is emphasized in color film. An olive complexion is best of all.

So much for looks. What about personality? I've been fortunate in working with girls who like the water. I want someone who isn't afraid to get wet—all wet, including hair. We start out on dry land but end completely soaked. Many times these are the best pictures. The summer months are perfect for this because the water is 70 degrees. In the winter months when we have some of our clearer skies, the air is cold and the water colder. Here is where those plastic bottles of hot water come in handy.

When we've exhausted the poses in which the model is not required to get wet and we finally arrive at the dreaded question "Do you mind getting wet?" we can offer, as a consolation, hot water which Alice pours over

Always preferring clear areas against which the model stands out, Peter Gowland poses Chris Holter lengthwise, having her approach the position carefully so that no footprints are evident. Backlighting with strobe fill. Daylight Diagram 7

Telltale footprints spoil an otherwise smooth background of sand against which model Diane Zapanta poses. High noon sun requires the head to be tipped far back to prevent harsh shadows on face. Daylight Diagram 2

By using the slanted section of sand and a high camera angle, we give model Jean Manson a clear area as a background for her bright-blue swimsuit and orange towel. Daylight Diagram 6

the trembling model. When she is posed at the edge of the water one would never guess that it was not the ocean that doused her. It's only possible to get a few exposures in this situation because the warm water runs out and the effect is short-lived as the cold air hits the wet body.

The most difficult time in photographing models is getting started. How to begin? The model and assistants are all waiting for the photographer to give commands. Sometimes it can be difficult, particularly in my case when I've used the beach to a point of exhaustion and find words sticking in my throat because I've said them so many times before. Luckily, I have Alice, who is able to step in when she sees this happening. She believes that it's best to get started at something, so she whips us all into action. In lieu of such a person I would suggest taking along clippings from magazines or books on glamour. I began selling "posing guides" several years ago for this purpose, and I find that they come in handy when I have a new model who is unfamiliar with my work. She looks through them and can often suggest a pose or situation herself.

The first pictures are never the best. It takes a while for everyone involved to coordinate and move along at the

Rock formations, while pretty to the naked
eye, can often be a distraction if used as an
entire background. Here, model Lisa Parks
is posed against a portion of rock but her
figure is easily outlined against the brighter
ocean reflections. Slight slant to pose
makes interesting composition. Daylight
Diagram 6

Low angle and leggy pose are natural to
jogger-model Diane Lienke. Daylight
Diagram 7

Diane Lienke's slim contoured body is posed with sun coming from ocean side. Water from receding wave has left sand free of footprints made when model approached setting. Daylight Diagram 2

same level. Knowing this, I prefer to begin with black-and-white film, using my Hasselblad or Pentax. If I am limited in time and am working on a color assignment that requires 4 x 5 or larger format, I begin by taking a 4 x 5 Polaroid. If the exposure is right we can continue without making another Polaroid until we change location or distance of camera to model. I always make two exposures of the same pose, for two reasons. First, the lab can develop one first and if for some reason the transparency is too light or too dark, the second can be corrected. Second, I like to have an extra picture or two to send to my overseas markets.

Generally I take six sheets of film at one location, varying the pose but keeping the camera at the same distance. Even though this may sound unspontaneous, I've found that being systematic produces a greater percentage of successful photographs.

Anyone who has followed my photography knows that my favorite lighting is sun behind the model. This effect is not only pleasing to the eye but makes it easier for the subject to keep from frowning.

Low afternoon sun, late in the day, gives nearly shadowless lighting to face of model Kathy McCullen. Not all models are able to look into the sun, requiring backlighting with strobe fill. Kathy is an exception. Daylight Diagram 2 (sun reversed)

This is why I work either early in the morning or late in the day—in order to have the sun in a low enough position to achieve this effect. I rarely work when the sun is directly overhead, at midday. As I mentioned, overhead sun creates problems with shadows that can only be corrected by putting a screen over the model. Filling in with flash does not always completely erase or fill in those dark shadows.

I look for something stationary, like a lifeguard tower or a pier where there is a shaded area. I place my camera in the shade, pose the model with the sun behind her and just at the edge of the shaded area. If necessary we extend a blanket over the camera and in back of me, in the absence of natural shade. The model is able to look into the darkened area, at the camera, even though she herself is sitting in a brightly lit portion of sand. Her eyes are bright, without frown wrinkles because she is looking into dark instead of light. The sun backlights her hair and I light her face with the Norman strobe.

Action in the surf during winter months is possible by using props that protect the model from being immersed. Here, a short ladder assists in emphasizing the shapely figure of model Nancy Li Brandi. Daylight Diagram 6

As I described earlier I test my strobe *before* use. I make a chart which I attach to the unit for easy reference. I pretest the strobe at different distances so that I am fairly sure of the results. The information taped to my strobe may read like this:

SMALL REFLECTOR NOT DIFFUSED

	f/4	f/5.6	f/8	f/11	f/16	f/22
50 *watt-sec.*	20 *ft.*	14 *ft.*	10 *ft.*	8 *ft.*	6 *ft.*	4½ *ft.*
100 *watt-sec.*	27 *ft.*	20 *ft.*	14 *ft.*	10 *ft.*	8 *ft.*	6 *ft.*
200 *watt-sec.*	30 *ft.*	25 *ft.*	20 *ft.*	12 *ft.*	9 *ft.*	7 *ft.*

I have a tape measure attached to the strap of the strobe unit and thus we can easily measure the distance, refer to the chart and save lots of time.

Even with this method I make Polaroid tests. The test allows for differences in the ambient light, the model's skin, and so on. It gives a starting place of known results without guesswork.

The longer I am in business the more I realize the importance of patience and attention to details. Many of my students have a basic desire and talent, but they are in a hurry and don't want to take a minute or two here and there to make tests or attend to details.

Each photographer has his own style. My particular trademark is carefully posing my models. Even in running pictures I encourage them to swing their arms in a particular manner and to try to cross their legs over slightly more than normal. This way the girl will look her very best without too much left to chance. We create spontaneity by the action of the water or her action. For example, when the model is posing on her knees in the surf every angle of her body is checked and arranged to the best advantage. No arms cutting into waistlines, hips turned slightly so as to keep them slim, bosom turned slightly toward sun to emphasize cleavage, hair away from face. Then we wait for the water to rush in, splash against her and give the impression of a candid picture.

Remember in running poses I take many exposures to get perhaps two or three perfect shots (but usually just one). If you recall, I prefocus at a particular spot, then have the model back up and run toward the camera. She doesn't have to be far back; about 10 feet from the camera. My eye is glued to my finder, and I watch the

The wet look during winter months is obtained by pouring hot water over model. Here, Joan Geletko is able to smile even though the air is cool because she knows there's more hot water waiting in the plastic bottle brought to the beach for that purpose.

action through that. I shoot when she's framed properly.

In working with surf and foam from the waves one must allow for the added reflection, sometimes as much as a stop difference in exposure.

After we have exhausted the use of the surf we look for other backgrounds that will lend themselves to working with a model. Sometimes pilings, fences, occasional playground equipment, logs, rocks.

Rocks are never in the right place, so we build our own. Here, model Kathy McCullen poses on fiberglass-coated form. Weight of her body holds "rock" in place. Daylight Diagram 6 (sun reversed)

Model Chris Holter kneels in the winter surf. Foam acts as a reflector, so adjustments to exposure must be made accordingly. Daylight Diagram 6

The problem with many of these is that the location is poor and the background is not clear. I've made myself a fake rock that I haul to the beach because the natural rocks are rarely isolated or else their best angle would require that the model face the sun. The fake rock works out well in the surf because the water helps to disguise its flaws!

By the time we have used as many backgrounds as possible, perhaps changed costume three times, everyone is losing energy and enthusiasm. It's best to quit and come back a different day, or take a break for the midday hours and continue for another hour in the afternoon when the sun is lower in the sky.

Not all models are able to strike such a becoming pose, but Camillia Hudson's dance training has given her the ability to extend her legs at this high angle even though the force of a wave crashes against her.

Dancers are among Peter Gowland's favorite subjects. Here model-dancer Camillia Hudson strikes a graceful pose before the breaking of an oncoming wave. Daylight Diagram 6

Model Debbie Shelton is caught as she walks gracefully through foam. Many exposures are necessary when action poses are taken in order to catch everything in pleasing composition. Daylight Diagram 6

Camillia Hudson doesn't mind the water when the temperature is in the 70s. Daylight Diagram 7

Karen Stride is posed to accentuate bustline and waist with anticipation of water to cover feet. Hasselblad. Daylight Diagram 6

Water has improved the picture by covering feet and lower legs and making pose look less contrived. Model, Karen Stride. Hasselblad. Daylight Diagram 6

Versatile model Karen Stride is equally lovely when posing nude. Finding a location with privacy is difficult. Here the background is near Malibu Beach. Daylight Diagram 6

Soft light of overcast day requires no additional light source for this photograph taken at Pirate's Cove, a nude-bathing section of beach near Los Angeles. Pentax. Overcast day

Peter directs model Chris Holter while assistant John Woodbury holds 36-inch Reflectasol (Larson super-silver). Reflectors are used to create backlight so the model does not have to face their brilliance.

For surf pictures where wave action is involved, model is posed first to accentuate waist and bustline. Arms should be away from body so as not to cover waistline. Model, Stephanie McLean. Hasselblad. Daylight Diagram 6

Working with models submerged in water is usually the last activity of the day. Here, Michelle Maddox reacts to the sudden wave of water that hits her reclining figure. Daylight Diagram 1

Anita Jackson holds a pre-positioned pose while the water swirls around her in soft foamy shapes. Daylight Diagram 1

A high angle is obtained by holding Hasselblad overhead in an attempt to eliminate distracting background. Actress, Melissa Prophet. Daylight Diagram 6

High angle with Melissa Prophet seated in shallow stream gives clear area as a background for her lovely figure. Daylight Diagram 6

A catamaran used as a prop to accentuate long shapely legs of Stephanie McLean. A yellow-green filter was used with Kodak Verichrome and with strobe fill. Daylight Diagram 6

Susanne Severeid keeps her figure trim and in good physical condition, for she is the top commercial nude model on the West Coast. Here, in the early-morning sun she is able to pose her body, clothed in shadows, as directed by Peter to emphasize line and curve. Daylight Diagram 3

Early-morning sun, low in the sky, gives side lighting to model-actress Susanne Severeid as she splashes in the tepid water. Daylight Diagram 3

One sure way to maintain enthusiasm for any type of creative work is to experiment, from time to time, with something completely different. A new direction is stimulating to both photographer and model, bringing a sense of excitement because one is never sure just what the result will be.

In any experimental work one needs the cooperation of the model. It is necessary to find someone who is amenable to working for a flat fee or in exchange for pictures rather than by the hour. If the idea is particularly appealing it is possible to elicit the interest of top-rate girls. Models never have enough pictures for their portfolios even when they're well established. The chance to break away from routine and participate in a creative venture with new pictures is frequently worth more than money.

Ideas for special effects can just pop into a photographer's head, or they can be suggested by a client, or a photograph or painting. I've gotten ideas from all of these. One very involved experiment which sounded easy was in striving for the look of oil as a background to the semi-nude model. Before hiring the six girls who were to be used in this project we wanted the approval of our client for the method we'd chosen. First I formed a 6-foot-square box. A piece of black plastic material was placed inside and over the edges of the box to contain the water, which we poured in to a depth of about an inch. Required format for the picture was to shoot from the waist up the model in a reclining position with hair fanning out around her head. The 72-inch Larson Reflectasol Hex was placed directly over the camera, but this didn't give us a reflection of her body. We added a direct Honeywell 880 slave, firing at the same instant as the strobe, which was placed on the floor to hit the side of her body but miss her face. In order to bring out a more oily look on the background we placed two Strobasols (directed through 36-inch Larson Translucents) at an angle to the side, and this lightened the very black area to the sides by reflecting these diffused screens in the water. We were pleased with the results but our client decided to go with the plastic alone, no water and no translucent reflections. Instead there was just the slight reflection of the body as created by the small direct Honeywell.

A similar effect, but with a different technique, was obtained for the background for some bathing-suit pic-

12

SPECIAL EFFECTS

I've always liked the combination of a pretty girl with water, and particularly a waterfall. To save time and money I decided to build a portable "waterfall" which could be moved according to the direction of the sun. Here, assistants Dean Cuadra with towel and Craig Harris prepare for the dumping of water on signal Daylight Diagram 9

Effect of complete water background, backlit by the sun on model Stephanie McLean. Daylight Diagram 9

tures in the studio. In front of our black paper roll background we hung a roll of orange plastic material, the type hung inside store windows to protect store interiors from glaring sun. I didn't purchase the roll—it was given to me—but I imagine any store with large window space would be able to give the name of the supplier.

A strobe was placed between the plastic and the black background, directed at the model's head. One large Hex was used from the camera's point of view. The reflection of the silver Hex against the plastic created wobbly light patterns, and an orange halo around the model's hair was produced by the strobe shooting through the orange plastic. The plastic roll which I can hang from a pole is handy for a variety of purposes and I've no doubt we'll think of another interesting way to use it.

Setup for multiple-image photograph showing the use of two Mylar mirrors (52 inches wide by 8 feet long) butted against each other at the bottom and creating an approximate 60-degree angle. Camera is placed at one end (shown at end of trough). Big umbrella shown was not used but instead the 42-inch Soff Box in center of picture was used from front, and the Honeywell 880 Strobonar shown in foreground lighted the background for model.

Wide-angle shot showing the position of the mirrors with assistants arranging the model's hair.

Multi-image of Susanne Gregard shows only one of several patterns possible by changing placement of the hands, head, etc. Bounce Indoor Diagram 19

The same two Mylar mirrors used again, this time in the vertical position with model Melonie Haller seated on white box. Assistant behind mirrors touched the Mylar at instant of exposure for irregular image. Bounce Indoor Diagram 6

Have you seen the Mylar material used for lightweight mirrors? It comes in rolls and I found it at a plastic mart. The width is 54 inches. I built two frame panels, both 52 inches wide and 6 feet tall. The Mylar was taped to these by using duct tape (sometimes called gaffer's tape),

Close-up showing multiple exposure into Mylar mirrors and model Melonie Haller wearing red sequined mask. Bounce Indoor Diagram 6

A stroboscopic effect can be had with an ordinary strobe light or a stroboscopic light which can be adjusted to a specific number of flashes per second. A special stroboscopic light was rented for this purpose. It's better to use one light source because the shadows are needed to separate the images. With ten exposures it is important to block the light from hitting the background, because it would receive ten times as much light as the subject. Direct Indoor Diagram 3

To bring an eye-catching element into this bathing-suit picture, reflection of two silver Reflectasols is caught in the sheet of orange plastic directly behind model Pamela La Grande. A second background of black paper roll is placed a few feet behind the orange plastic. A single light, placed between the two backgrounds, hits the model's head from behind. Bounce Indoor Diagram 20

which can be purchased at a hardware store or plumbing-supply house. One should wear white cotton gloves to keep fingerprints from marring the Mylar. When it is stretched taut it is impossible to tell the difference between it and a glass mirror.

Our model was seated, nude, on a white box situated in the corner where the two mirrored panels joined. We posted a third person in back of the Mylar and directed him to jiggle the image by touching the back surface lightly, distorting the perfect reflections. In order to have color reflected in strange patterns we hung brightly colored materials over light stands next to the camera and pieces of colored chiffon over the translucent reflectors through which our strobes were directed.

At a different time the same framed Mylar mirrors produced a kaleidoscopic effect. We braced the two panels together in a V shape and placed them on 3-foot-high stools, holding them in place with a light stand on either side. The camera was situated at one end and the model at the other. The lens picked up the multiple images and the slightest variation of hands, arms, or body positions created a new pattern. At one point our model lowered herself putting her head in the center of the V. A vase of flowers was placed in back of her head so that only the flowers showed above, producing a burst of color coming out of her head!

For a touch of humor we used these same panels with a nude model, placing her against the straight edge of the one panel so that it bisected her body exactly in two. By raising one leg she gave the impression of a leaping figure. The lightweight frame is easily steadied by the hidden leg and arm. Endless variations are possible.

Working with mirrored surfaces requires that attention be paid to the lighting and to placement of the mirrors so that the reflected image is plain and does not include the camera or whatever else is in the room. In using strobe lights one has to make sure that there will be no glare. A Polaroid test will tell whether or not either of these problems exists.

Use of multiple exposures brings another creative avenue to the glamour photographer. Multiple exposures can be obtained in the darkroom, in the camera and with the use of stroboscopic lights. These are expensive items but can be rented. Usually they have a control for the number of flashes per second. I hired a dancer to run across the plane of the film while the light flashed several times. Only one strobe light is necessary and is really better than multiple light sources because of the many images being repeated on top of one another. I brought the light in from the side and had the model run toward it. If the light had come from the front position all the images would have seemed to run together. Shadows are necessary with stroboscopic lighting.

It's possible to do this type of shot with a regular strobe and manual operation but this would not be as consistent. One could also achieve a similar effect by a series of exposures having the model change poses slightly, moving away from her original position each time. For action the stroboscopic light is best. The camera should be on a tripod with the lens open during the entire cycle.

No light should be directed toward the background, since the multiple exposures would wipe out the dark color. That is another reason for placing the light to one side of the subject rather than directing it from the front. The only place where this would not happen would be outdoors at night on top of a building where only the sky

Triple image is created in darkroom by moving the paper after each exposure.

is visible. The sky would not reflect back into the camera as a studio background would.

Use of a large net, 6 feet square for portraits and 12 feet square (or larger) for full-lengths, creates an unusual background for outdoor situations. The net is placed between subject and background so that it acts as a diffuser for any distracting foliage, etc. I have seen this done by a Japanese photographer and it was difficult to tell what medium he had used just by looking at the photograph.

Diffusion can be obtained by the use of grease on glass. Vaseline is rubbed onto a piece of glass, which can be 4 x 5 or 5 x 7. This is held in front of the lens. It's wise to allow a small spot in the center to be free of vaseline.

With sun as backlight, background structures remain dark and unidentifiable because of long lens. Model, Janet Larsen. Daylight Diagram 6

Same setting with window screen held in back of model to diffuse any distracting structures in background. Model, Janet Larsen. Daylight Diagram 6

Thus the edges of the picture are softened but the faces are sharp.

Smoke machines, of the type used in commercials or motion pictures, are excellent for scenes in which one wants to have the look of a misty morning or evening. These machines can be rented for a day or a week. They can be used indoors as well as out. They are rather noisy and the smoke can arouse the suspicions of the fire department, so plans to avoid interruption should be made before attempting to use one.

Printing one negative on top of another permits one to obtain a scenic effect right in the darkroom. I have series of cloud negatives, of tree limbs against a white sky, of birds. All of these have been used more than once to improve an otherwise plain picture.

I've always liked the combination of water and glamour. My studio is close to the ocean and to nearby streams and waterfalls. Yet the one picture I'd thought of for many years I've still not found possible: a model with a sheet of falling water as her background. I decided to build a waterfall myself. I used wood to construct a

With sun backlighting model Janet Larsen and use of 150mm lens on Hasselblad, the background is diffused but light. Daylight Diagram 17

Assistant Craig Harris and Alice Gowland hold piece of window screen behind model to diffuse house in background. Daylight Diagram 6

Use of Leon Vignetter Pro II #1 darkens the background at edges of picture. Daylight Diagram 17

Use of Leon Vignetter 02-G creates an obvious circle with dark edges. Daylight Diagram 17

Use of Leon Vignetter 02-TR creates white edges, leaving portrait area inside of diffused circle. Daylight Diagram 17

Use of Vaseline rubbed onto a piece of glass and placed in front of lens. Vaseline is applied in a circle with clear area in middle, giving diffusion to edge of picture with no definite shape to diffusion. One can experiment with various amounts and shapes. Daylight Diagram 17

trough measuring 8 feet long and 8 inches deep and hinged this to a set of braces 8 feet high on each end. A large wooden handle to control the tipping was nailed to one end of the trough. Since it was collapsible I could transport it anywhere. First I made tests using it in the patio. The trough was filled with water from our garden hose. At a given signal, my assistant pulled on the wooden handle, spilling the water in an 8-foot sheet behind the model. We found that the water patterns varied when we tipped the trough from slow to fast. Being able to see through the sheet of water gives the picture an unreal feeling, because waterfalls rarely have any great depth behind them! You can see the result of this experiment on page 191.

Suzanne Severeid poses in wet sand. Use of star filter causes sparkling highlights. Sun backlight creates pattern as reflection. Daylight Diagram 1

*The rushing tide and white foam create
highlights from sun backlighting figure.
Star filter creates spectacular burst where
sun is at its brightest. Daylight Diagram 1*

Model is posed outside, leaning against frosted-wired glass. A reflector is placed near her feet to bounce sunlight into her face. Daylight Diagram 11 (diagram shows subject in front of background but our subject and the reflector were placed behind glass background)

Picture of model in kneeling pose taken at a previous time is printed, mounted on thin cardboard and carefully cut out. It is then nested in a basket of real strawberries. Lighting used on the strawberries with girl in basket is the same as was used on the original picture of the girl: main light at camera right, hair light camera left and to rear. Thus the same shadows are cast on the berries. Bounce Indoor Diagram 11

We had an oversized champagne glass and printed a picture of a model to fit the glass. (An ordinary-size glass could have been used with the picture being printed smaller.) The picture of the girl was held in position by a wire taped against the rear rim of glass, with the camera angle hiding it from view. Alice took picture of Peter with model to show relationship of size and for a more dramatic effect. Bounce Indoor Diagram 11

Model was first photographed on plain white background in studio, shooting up toward seamless ceiling. Cloud negative was pulled from the files. (1) Place negative of picture of girl in enlarger and trace her image on a piece of ordinary paper. (2) Put cloud negative in enlarger and trace it on same paper in position desired. (3) Make a test strip of cloud negative to arrive at proper exposure. (4) Print cloud negative but do not develop. Write exposure on the back (this gives you a starting place should you have to reprint the picture) and place in a covered box. (5) Place negative of girl in enlarger, using tracing paper for placement, and make a test strip to arrive at the proper exposure. (6) Take first paper with cloud exposure, place it under the enlarger and make exposure of girl. Develop. An interesting fact is that the cloud negative and girl negative when printed alone will have good contrast but when printed together will have a flat look, perhaps by as much as one paper grade. Thus the girl alone was printed on number 3 paper and cloud alone on number 4. The combined printing was on grade number 4. Cloud was exposed at f/16 for 4 seconds and the girl at f/11 for 4 seconds. Bounce Indoor Diagram 14

The nonreflective black background was obtained by using soft fabric similar to velvet but lighter in weight, rather than the black-paper roll. Two backlights were placed at 45-degree angles directed toward the model. These were screened from hitting the lens by two go-bo's. A hair light was used above the model. The main light (a 17-inch Larson Soff Box) was placed on the floor approximately where the fire would be. A sheet of yellow tissue paper was taped over the light. Polaroid tests were taken with both the Hasselblad and the 4 x 5 Gowlandflex to determine the lighting and exposure. To double expose with the Hasselblad it was necessary to remove the magazine after making the exposure of the girl, then wind the shutter and replace the magazine for the exposure of the fire. Owners of 35mm cameras will have to make composite shots when printing, using two negatives. While model was still in studio, we moved to the fireplace where a fire was photographed. We hung black cloth around the fireplace, exposing the fire area only. We were able to place the fire in the exact position because the groundglass had been marked with grease pencil to indicate the model's feet position. Exposure on the model was with electronic flash 1/60 second at f/16; the exposure for the fire was f/5.6 1/60 second, using a tripod. Bounce Indoor Diagram 12

A texturing screen was used in the darkroom to give an etched look to this figure study. The grain is more obvious in the shadow areas. It was necessary to print the negative alone for 4 seconds, then with the screen for 5 seconds. Every negative is different, so one has to make tests to determine the possible effects. Direct Indoor Diagram 2

Index